Other Books by Jack E. Dunning

Nymphomania Bloodlust

Short Stories

Snuffy's Last Walk
Janina's Legacy
Deadly Cloudburst
Drizzle's Death
The Mystery of the Arizona Pyramid
Partners in Road Rage

WITHOUT THE LAMPSHADE

How I Learned to Love my Brown Martini

Jack E. Dunning

2D4 Press
Cave Creek, Arizona

I have tried to recreate events, locales and conversations from my memories of them. In order to maintain their anonymity in some instances I have changed the names of individuals and places, I may have changed some identifying characteristics and details such as physical properties, occupations and places of residence.

First edition printing
ISBN-9780692704745

This book is affectionately dedicated to my wife who has made all my writing possible, and without whom I could never have kicked the bad habits of drinking and smoking.

CHAPTER CONTENTS

Chapter One: The Beginning and the End

It all came to an abrupt halt one dreary Sunday morning almost 35 years ago. It was raining and I was looking out the window of our twelfth floor high-rise in College Park, Maryland, trying to settle my stomach after another night of non-stop drinking and smoking. This had been going on for over twenty years and I had gotten very good at it. Yes, booze and cigarettes had become my comfort zone. Nevertheless, I had just decided to give up both of these nasty habits…cold turkey.

Deserting the pair simultaneously, all in one day and really with no remorse. It had been years of hard and serious boozing, starting with the Southern special, bourbon and coke, moving on later to the more sophisticated Scotch on the rocks. And in between there had been almost every other kind of libation known to man.

As I looked at the wooded park across from the apartments, I gulped down the last of my "Cockroach," a drink I had invented to ward off the DTs and convince my stomach I had nothing against it. It worked. A simple concoction consisting of V-8 (not tomato juice), Worcestershire Sauce, and plenty of Tabasco.

My problem was I *liked* the taste of Scotch, consuming so much that I eventually had to switch to wine to protect my liver; or at least that's what I told myself. The night before I had polished off one-half gallon of Rhine wine and smoked four packs of cigarettes. I picked the Rhine because it was dry, and had switched to one of those low tar smokes you had to drop to your knees to get a good drag.

Earlier in my life when living in Iowa, I paid the required annual visit to my internist—who was well aware of my drinking habits—and he laid it out point blank. I was exclaiming what good shape I thought I was in, despite my voracious imbibing. His quick reply with absolutely no hesitation was, "If you keep this up it's going to kill you."

I thought about that later at my favorite Des Moines Bar after two Scotch/rocks. I decided to get a second opinion so I asked—let's call him Bennie—the owner and bartender. I don't know what I expected but it wasn't what I was looking for. Also quite familiar with my cavorting with the spirits, he agreed with my doc.

So went another evening of high jinx with friends that drank almost as much as I did. I used to quip when we would all head for our favorite watering hole: "Hey, let's hurry up and get drunk." One can only wonder about the reasoning behind that kind of thinking that once landed me in a stranger's backyard under a chicken coop. I never did learn why people were allowed to keep chickens in this upscale Des Moines neighborhood. Pigs maybe, but not chickens.

It was, in fact, Des Moines, Iowa, where I really learned to drink, working for a large publishing conglomerate. When first being interviewed for the job, having just been introduced to the martini and after my second one, they made me an offer. In my condition, it was necessary to excuse myself and go to the bathroom before answering. I had to sit on the "john," without purpose, except to use my pen and a piece of toilet paper to figure whether they were offering me more money than I was making at the time. They were, just barely.

Actually, I had my first drink when I was about five, when we were living in Paducah, Kentucky, my parents giving me a sip during their parties. What they didn't know was that I was making the rounds of all the guests, my intake probably adding up to a good-sized cocktail. Even in those days, I could hold my liquor.

Being the only kid in the crowd, nobody wanted to talk to me, so I created my own imaginary friend. Joe lived in the closet of our apartment, and even though my parents were a little concerned when they heard me talk about him, they figured it was healthy for me to have an active imagination. Although that active imagination would survive the years, my buddy, Joe, would desert me over a disagreement.

Of course, I was the only one who could see Joe, and I was the only one Joe would talk to. When I couldn't be found, it was understood that I was in the closet commiserating with Joe. I have never had a more responsive listener in my life than Joe, except for my wife, Barbara.

In later years it was impossible to rekindle my relationship with Joe when I needed to discuss my hangovers and why I had done the bizarre things that had led up to these post-inebriation after-effects. Joe was my closet analyst and understood my childhood needs, but when it came to my ludicrous adult drinking habits, he just simply disowned me. A move I fully understand today.

Before I decided to get into the religion business, which I will explain later, I was a happy guy in high school with friends who also liked to drink. They were attracted either to my bad habits or I to theirs.

Jackson, Tennessee, was basically my hometown. In high school, I almost took off with a carnival that came to town, which could indicate a Gypsy pattern always there in my personality. You cannot understand the gypsy urge unless you have lived with it. Not even sure today how much my infatuation with one of the showgirls named Fifi had to do with my contemplated departure, but I can tell you she was a looker.

Fifi was really French, at least that's what she told me, beautiful, probably in her mid-twenties, and one evening took me back to her dressing room after the show. She asked me if there was anything she could do for me, and spying a bottle of bourbon on her table, I said "a drink." It was tragic what I missed out on because of my fascination with booze.

Jackson was kind of a hick town; as a matter of fact, it had a suburb named Hicksville. There was a fast food place there that had carhops, all black in the late 1940s, and my drinking buddies and I frequented the place because we could order cokes and mix it with our bourbon in a plain brown bag. Thomas, our regular server, caught us in the act one night with the comment, "86 on that."

3

Thomas refused to serve us in the future, making sure all his waiter-friends also ignored us. We simply went to another drive-in and made sure to keep the spirits hidden when we ordered the coke. Now at this age there is no way of knowing when an adult like Thomas was telling you something that you should listen to, much less how his advice may affect your future.

We had two national fraternities in high school: Sigma Phi Omega (SPO), and Theta Kappa Omega (TKO). I was invited to join both but chose the SPOs, simply because most of my buddies were joining. I had to learn the Greek alphabet and still remember it to this day.

A fraternal organization binds together its membership in a common purpose that allows them to speak and act as a group. We did this by throwing wild parties in our designated meeting room behind a member's house, and I will never understand why the adults did not catch us in our drunken antics.

I was so smashed when I returned home one night from an SPO party that I fell asleep on our space heater situated between the front door and my room. It was winter and in use. There were vents on the top, much like those on air vents in current homes, and when I woke up the next morning in my bed, I looked like I had been barbecued. My dear mother had quietly moved me off what could have eventually produced 3rd degree burns.

The fraternities had annual dances every summer where you dated up and both of you dressed to the hilt for the gala. I had just broken up with my longtime girlfriend, but managed to strong-arm one of the most popular gals in school to go with me. I wasn't the best dancer and she was excellent, so the evening was a challenge with me in the mood I was in.

After several drinks, my dance floor agility improved dramatically and the two of us were even enjoying ourselves. But once I get started with the booze, there is no slowing me down, so I was relatively plastered when the dance was over. My date and I were descending the steps of the Jackson Country Club when I, by then almost completely impaired with the wobblies, stepped on the back of her formal and pulled the front right off her boobs.

Everyone rushed to cover her up but me, because at that point I had almost reached oblivion.

While still in high school, I had a job with the local newspaper, *The Jackson Sun*, as a photographer and the engraver of the metal plates that were used in those days to reproduce pictures in the newspaper. My friend worked right next door for a dental lab, so we both headed to work together each afternoon after school.

Both of our bosses did their share of drinking but one of the partners my friend worked for had a unique way of really announcing it. When he said, "I'm going to the river…" we knew we wouldn't see him for several days. He did go to a river cabin just outside of town, and spent his time there just drinking. His family knew he would eventually run out of booze and come home.

My friend's other partner made no such announcement, rather, he just left work in the afternoon, picked up his girlfriend—he was married with children—and headed for his favorite drinking joint, armed with his favorite booze for the evening. The law looked the other way in Jackson, so you just brought your bottle in and ordered "set-ups."

Sometimes he never made it out of his office; his "date" came to him. This usually happened when the partner was at the river. She was taller than this guy, had a great body, and was unbelievably stacked. After I was initially introduced to her, she never uttered another word in my presence. Just a grin that indicated she enjoyed what she was about to do.

Chapter Two: Growing Up Real Fast

One night when I was working late at the newspaper, I heard this heavy pounding next door, and went to check it out. When you entered the dental lab, there was a long counter where they did business with customers. On this particular evening, a piece of cardboard had been placed on the floor in front of the counter, with several work smocks thrown over it for cushioning.

The partner was on top of his girlfriend on this makeshift mattress, and when I walked in to the office, they didn't miss a beat. Now I'm still a high school kid, perpetually horny, and not about to pass up a chance to experience some live, homemade porno. They probably wouldn't have even noticed me, but in a few minutes I became too jealous to hang around any longer. I went back to work but found it near impossible to keep my mind on what I was doing.

Many a time my friend or I received a call from this partner's wife begging us to go get him and bring him home. We did, and he never argued about it, even though many times he was still in the drinking stage and most likely hadn't reached the point where he had exerted his masculinity, which must have been considerable, based on his shenanigans. However, in one horrible moment it would all end in tragedy.

One particular evening I was called out by the newspaper to photograph an automobile accident just outside Jackson where there had been fatalities. After calling the medics, the Jackson cops always called me next. I was blown away; it was our Casanova with his favorite girlfriend…both dead…wound around a tree.

I got there before the ambulance, and even though it was pretty obvious the two were gone, the cops were doing their best to see if anything could be done. I did what I could to help, and was at least able to identify the bodies. Although the medics couldn't pronounce them dead, they did confirm they had died in the collision with the tree. I had to shoot the scene for the paper, but made sure no identification could be made in the photographs. I asked the police to withhold names until I could notify the family.

Highway disasters around this small town were more numerous than you might expect, partly due to the fact that you weren't able to go into a restaurant or bar and buy a drink. You had to buy a bottle, usually a fifth, and hide it while drinking, so most were inclined to finish it off before the end of the evening. It took years for these dry regions to realize they were killing off their citizens.

In yet another devastating auto accident I was again called to a familiar highway where a repeat of what I had experienced so many times had happened again. A drunk had hit a couple in an oncoming car head-on, pinning them in the car. I got to the location within minutes from where I lived and immediately smelled gasoline. I had done this enough to know what the inevitable result would be.

I helped others desperately trying to free the two people, but all the doors were jammed, and they were pinned under parts of the dashboard. With the fire department on the way, we were racing against time. All of a sudden the car burst into flames, and we focused on just getting the occupants out. I could see the two innocent passengers who were screaming for help, but there was nothing we could do.

They were hopelessly wedged in and soon we had to just back away and watch as they burned to death. Several of the rescuers actually vomited on the highway. I covered the story for *The Jackson Sun*. As bad as this was, it wasn't enough to always keep me from driving after drinking, but when I did it, was one-eyed-slow with extreme care. It did work for me, but this is no excuse for driving when drunk.

Jackson was actually a "dry" town, if you can believe that, which meant you could not buy liquor there legally. But getting it was no problem, since bootleggers had all you wanted…at a price. You could even have it delivered to your house—of course at an additional premium—but my father chose to go to them. They were housed in a modern building just outside the city limits, in the county, and my dad often took me with him to make a run.

The first time I couldn't believe my eyes. Inside the structure, all the liquor was in a large concrete square in the center of the room about one foot deep. Hanging overhead was a huge concrete block sized to fit in the space below. If the place was raided, all they had to do was hit a button that released the block that crushed all the booze. The bootlegger couldn't be arrested without evidence of at least one full bottle.

On the other hand, there was a homemade remedy that you could buy from the people who brewed it in the Tennessee backcountry. They were called "moonshiners," and their product was "white lightning." They had a very unique distribution system, and it did not include you coming to them for the product.

If you like folk tales, there are hundreds when talking about this Southern delicacy. Many have been passed down from generation to generation, and some don't make the folks from the Volunteer State so proud. Two of these tales I can recount from personal experience, and they are both true. But first, some background.

One of the ways white lightning was fermented was by using embalming fluid. That could kill you. But the good stuff had a cloudy sediment in the bottom called the "mother" that the experienced corn whiskey—another of its names—drinker knew to look out for. There were stills all over the hills of Tennessee, and, unfortunately, I once almost ran into one by mistake. You don't want to do that if you want to live.

Just to give you an idea of the dangers wrought in sneaking up on one of these contraptions, the Lost Dutchman's Mine in the Superstition Mountains of Arizona may claim its victims, but I will bet almost as many have resulted from people innocently running into a Tennessee moonshiner's still. As the saying goes, you never know what hit you.

I was on assignment from *The Jackson Sun* to investigate a family that claimed they had spotted a black panther close to their house. Although some folks thought these animals did dwell in the hills of Tennessee, no one had ever confirmed seeing one. Until now. I headed into the hills and upon arriving at the location found an authentic *Tobacco Road*.

The entire family was sitting on the front porch, the father and mother on a couch that had seen its best days twenty years ago. A daughter and son that looked to be in their teens were sitting on the steps with an old bird dog that looked underfed. They were accompanied by an old wringer washing machine and a rusted refrigerator...open. They didn't say a word until I said hello.

It still wasn't hello. The father replied, "You the guy from the newspaper?" I acknowledged, and without a word he left the porch and started into the woods.

Not knowing what I was supposed to do, I just stood there and waited. Pretty soon the wife said, "Ain't you gonna follow him?" Now I knew what to do.

After ten or fifteen minutes of crashing through the underbrush with a 4X5 Speed Graphic in my hand, the guy allowed as how this was the place he had seen the panther. It was a clearing and there was no animal of any kind anywhere to be seen. Not knowing what the next move was, I asked him if the plan was to just wait. He answered telling me the panther only came out at night. It was three o'clock in the afternoon.

Although I wanted to ask him "What the hell are we doing here now?" I didn't. He just stood there and looked at me until I shrugged to indicate what's next? "Guess you could look around over there, that's where he come from," was the reply. My gut feeling now was this man had seen something in the night, probably more like a shadow, and just wanted to tell his neighbors he was interviewed by the newspaper.

I decided to take a quick jaunt into the woods to satisfy him, then wrap it up and go home. Starting out in the opposite direction he had pointed to, my guide said, "Wouldn't go that way if I was you." I immediately got suspicious, and my investigative juices kicked in. It was now imperative that I had to see whatever I shouldn't. I proceeded but noted he did not follow.

After several yards through more brush, all of a sudden a man popped out of a dense area with a shotgun pointed right at me. I could see smoke behind him. He said, "Ain't nairn here you need. Git." He had a look on his face that told me he wouldn't hesitate to use the gun. "Take yairn camera and git." With my speed graphic in hand, a quick decision was made to do exactly what the man told me.

Chapter three: Riding the Rails for Booze

I had almost run across a moonshiner's' still and in this part of the country that is a capital offense, often punishable by death if you actually see the distillery itself, the person operating it, and looked anything like a revenuer. My best guess tells me the guy with the gun was in a particularly good mood that day, thus, my fortunate luck. I hurried away, and all the panther spotter said to me was, "I told you so."

While still in high school there was a guy, a fraternity brother, who drove around in a panel truck with no windows, but with a mattress in the back. While hanging around with him I found out what the mattress was for when he asked me to drive one night after picking up his girlfriend.

The two of them promptly headed for the back of the truck, and I was instructed to drive...anywhere. You have no idea how hard it is to navigate with that kind of moaning going on. What one won't do for a frat brother. We drove around for over an hour until he finished his business and I was so horny I could barely drive. He may have been a frat brother, but he didn't offer me sloppy seconds.

But there was also another reason for the panel truck other than secret sex. My friend was a bootlegger on wheels, selling white lightning as well as the regular stuff. He removed side panels in the rear of the truck and filled the walls with booze. One night I was out with him on deliveries and the cops caught us speeding.

They had an idea this guy was bootlegging, but had never actually caught him. We lost them in his souped up Ford panel, but it was necessary for this guy to make some moves that almost topped the ones made by Steve McQueen's car chase in the movie, *Bullitt*.

There was one more incident with white lightning, but minus the moonshiners. My father got me a job when I was in high school working with the railroad's track maintenance gang. They were the ones who maintained the tracks on which the trains ran. All black but me. Since I was the son of a railroad executive, the gang knew they had to watch out for me. They were like a good waiter, hovering to provide the best of service but very inconspicuous.

One of them was named Charlie, who was no bigger than I was, but his body was capable of doing things equal to other workers twice his size. They all looked up to Charlie, although he was not actually a supervisor. Charlie was extremely street-smart and he took me under his wing. If Charlie thought I shouldn't do something, nobody questioned his decision, including the gang boss.

But on to the new encounter with white lightning, which, of course, Charlie was also involved with. In those days the railroads used something called a handcar or pump car, which was the width of the tracks and square, with four metal wheels under a platform, allowing it to travel on the rails just like a train. It was powered by two men pumping see-saw-like handles that were tied into a gear mechanism that made it move.

The handcar was used primarily to visually check the condition of the rails, and could easily be lifted on and off the rails by four men. One day Charlie called me and said we are going to make an inspection of the line for a ten-mile portion leading out of Jackson, Tennessee. I would accompany him and three others, but was not allowed to help them place the car on or off the rails. Nor was I allowed to do any pumping.

We were tooling along when we suddenly stopped and Charlie got off the car and went over to a power pole along the railroad's right-of-way. He removed some loose dirt around the pole and came up with what looked like a bottle with liquid in it. We made nine more stops like this and for the life of me I don't know how Charlie knew at which pole to stop, but he did with meticulous precision.

Each bottle was wiped clean and placed in a paper bag with the maintenance tools. I couldn't stand it and asked Charlie what the hell was in the bottles. His answer: white lightning for several of the railroad executives, and one bottle for him. The moonshiners had left them there the night before, knowing Charlie and his crew would collect them this day. It was a unique distribution system, but it worked.

All the guys had a drink and I was shocked when Charlie asked me if I wanted a swig. I took one, and it was the smoothest tasting booze I have ever had in my life. Yes, it had the "mother" sediment in the bottom and it went down as easy as drinking water, but oh, so much better tasting. This stuff ranged in those days from fifty to eighty percent alcohol and if you weren't careful, it could put the lights out real quick..

As Charlie requested, I never told my dad, but looked around the house the next week for his stash. Either he hadn't ordered any or had a hiding place even I couldn't find. Most likely, the latter. Once when we were planning a fraternity party I went to Charlie for a couple of bottles, which he wouldn't let me pay for, and they were the hit of the evening.

Jackson was also the first place I ever smoked pot. I was with two older friends, and we were working a roadhouse on the outside of town. One was the bouncer, the other was the doorman, and I was the photographer. All the men there were with someone else's wife, so no one really wanted their picture taken but I persisted, coming up with a library of photographs I would later discover could have been very valuable.

I bummed a cigarette from one of my buddies and after a few minutes I was the happiest one there, except I didn't know why. This was in the late 1940s when the street term for marijuana was "reefer," and when they told me that's what I had just smoked, I still didn't know what it was. It would be several years before I tried that again.

The South wasn't the most bustling place to grow up in, but it did provide some interesting experiences that you didn't find in other parts of the country. There was a saying then—maybe even today— that there are only three things to do for excitement in Jackson on Saturdays: one, go watch haircuts; two, check out the produce trucks unloading; and three, have sex. I opted for the latter.

But, somewhere in my senior year of high school I got religion; actually not the authentic kind, as I would discover later. It was enough to get me closely involved with the Methodists, and the assignment of three churches in the backwoods around Jackson. These were the places that established ministers didn't want. I also entered Lambuth College in Jackson as a pre-ministerial student, and was fascinated with the study of religion. Still am.

However, there was a restlessness I just couldn't explain. Becoming a preacher just didn't seem to fit. It was pretty obvious and my professors agreed, as not one of them discouraged me from leaving school. I had the feeling there was something waiting out there that I was meant to do, but had no idea how many years it would take to get there. I would wake up decades later lamenting over the fact that I hadn't followed my nose from the beginning to start putting down words on paper.

After leaving the religion business, I made the decision to join the Navy and get married. Both of these announcements caused no end to my parents' already strong concerns that I had no idea what I wanted to do. I never did let them know just how right they almost were, and they probably wouldn't have understood if I had told them I wanted to write. I left Jackson on a train a few days later for Great Lakes boot training.

These few weeks are a part of my life I could have done without. It was wet and cold, plus taking orders are not conducive to my mental make-up. Once when I called my M-1 rifle a "gun" in front of the old Chief Petty Officer that had been recalled to train us recruits, he said, "Sailor, sleep with your gun for a week." When I inquired why, he added, "Change that to two weeks."

But at least getting out of this basic training soon was inevitable; getting out of the Navy would take another four annoying and excruciating years. There would be some high points, but most of them were on the low end. Thank God I had already learned how to drink so all I had to do was pick up where I left off in high school, but unfortunately there would be none of that in boot camp. Eventually I left Great Lakes for more school in sunny Jacksonville, Florida.

Chapter Four: Sunshine, Palm Trees and More Religion

Jacksonville was uneventful except for an incident at a whorehouse. I met some friends at the Naval Air Base there from Jackson, Tennessee, and naturally we had to go out and get plastered. I ended up obliterated, passed out in this den of iniquity, and don't remember anything after that. But I do vaguely recall before the darkness settled several barely dressed women seductively walking around me. You can see how out of it I was because I don't remember being the least bit aroused.

The next day in class I asked a buddy, who had been with me the night before, exactly what happened. He said that he and the other two guys chose girls and proceeded to take care of business. Concerned, because I had just gotten married before going into the Navy, I asked what I had done. He said the madam inquired which girl I wanted and my reply was, "I only do it for love."

I am still a romantic, but that philosophy was challenged in later years.

My first wife, who was pregnant at the time, joined me in Jacksonville to have the baby, since the Navy would pay for everything. She took a train ride down because that was all we could afford. We found an apartment off base and I commuted to the school daily. We were actually enjoying ourselves as it was the first time either of us had been to Florida. And then the big day came for my first daughter to be born, which was all normal, thankfully.

But while she was still in the hospital there was a character like the one who played Maxwell Q. Klinger in the *MASH* TV series. If you recall, Klinger would dress up as a woman to try to convince the Army he was crazy so they would discharge him. Our guy was much more creative. In the same hospital as my wife, he would walk out of his room several times a day, in his hospital gown, get on an old motorcycle that didn't run which was propped against the side of the building.

He would simulate starting it by pushing the kick-starter, complete with his sound effects, then sit for close to an hour, now making noises like an engine running. We never learned if he got his discharge, but I gave the concept consideration, since I was completely disenchanted with the Navy, even at this early stage. I've said it before but it's worth repeating for those mavericks like me. I was not meant to take orders, so this should be taken into consideration for anyone thinking about joining the military.

Following the Jacksonville prep school, it was on to Key West, Florida, for several weeks' training in underwater guided missiles. The barracks I was assigned to was right next to where they beached the PBM seaplanes. A PBM (long out of use in the Navy) did not have its own wheels, making it necessary, after landing in the water, to taxi up to a ramp where wheels were attached for land.

One day a group of us from the school was watching them beach one of the PBMs. Once the wheels were attached, the plane was towed up the ramp by a tractor and down the tarmac to where it would be secured. There was a man on the side of each wheel during the towing. The guy on the port side looked very wobbly and it was confirmed later that he had been drinking.

As we watched in horror, this same guy somehow got his foot caught under the front of the wheel and it whipped his body around where it slammed him to the ground and over 33,000 lbs. of seaplane literally flattened the guy on the concrete. The crew, obviously stunned, shut down the operation and immediately called the medics. None of us went to dinner that evening.

During my stay in Key West I tried all the bars, especially Kilroy's, where a lot of the locals hung out and it was said that Ernest Hemingway sometime frequented. The writer had a home in Key West where he lived and wrote for ten years, producing books such as "A Farewell to Arms" and "To Have and Have Not," whose locale was Key West. Hemingway's cats were still at his home, leading me to believe, along with a later experience covered here, writers preferred the calming effect of felines.

I soon tired of the bar scene—that restlessness again—and spent more time hanging around the barracks and talking to the guys, and somehow the fact that I once had ministerial training came up. All of a sudden a bunch of guys became interested in religion. Two actually asked me to help them with their failing faith and abruptly I began to take on the mantle of preacher-man again, and it thoroughly shocked me that I not only enjoyed it but, at the time, craved doing more. So I did.

Getting off my shift at the base one afternoon, I walked into Key West after searching the phone book for the closest Methodist church. I found it after walking a few streets and getting lost several times. Entering the open sanctuary through the front door, I immediately spied a man that just looked like he would be the minister. He was, and introduced himself as James Harvest, not his real name, and the meeting was the beginning of a six-month—my remaining time in school—relationship I enjoyed greatly.

After we had talked for some time and he learned of my ministerial background training, he asked me if I would be interested in participating in Sunday services, of course, when I did not have base duty. I quickly accepted, and that was yet another revival in my involvement in the business of religion. My duties were to help James on Sunday where after a few weeks he actually asked me to deliver the sermon. I was petrified. I harkened back to the three churches in Jackson but knew this would be different.

Everything turned out well enough, but it was obvious the congregation didn't put me on a level with their regular pastor. It was even more evident at the door of the church as I thanked them for coming. Maybe this is why my second calling didn't take any better hold than the first but I was determined, and stuck with it until leaving Key West. One thing is for sure, it kept me out of the bars. The interesting part was the fact that, during this period of fellowship, I didn't miss drinking. Go figure.

The parsonage was right behind the church and I hung out there a lot with the Harvest family, which included Mrs. Harvest and two daughters. I was treated like a son and began to get a guilt trip, as more and more I was getting that same feeling again that the Religion business wasn't for me. And then James Harvest threw me a bombshell. He was going to a conference out of state and would be gone Friday through Sunday. James wanted me to take over the Sunday services while he was gone.

At first I wondered if this was a sign, then decided I really hadn't changed in the last few days and it was simply a coincidence. But I had no intention of letting the pastor down, so I said yes and began to prepare for my big day. Fortunately, the choir director, who was a transplant from New York, could sense my anxiety and provided some support; not sure whether my angst was my lack of conviction or just the fear of preparing and carrying out the service on my own.

Regardless, it too came off well enough, though crowd reaction to me remained about the same. James returned and the next time we met he told me I had a good future in the ministry. I didn't disagree and actually never did tell him that I had real doubts about becoming a minister. I only corresponded with James Harvest once after leaving Key West and soon after completely lost touch. I learned later that James and his family had left the Old Stone Church in Key West and moved to Jacksonville.

One thing that happened before I left, a film company was making the film, "Beneath the 12-Mile Reef," in Key West and contracted to use the church parsonage as the location for several scenes. The film starred Robert Wagner, Terry Moore and Gilbert Roland, and I was allowed to hang around during the filming. But the real action wasn't on the set but rather on the front lawn of the resort hotel where the cast was staying. Crowds gathered to watch the two young stars cavort around on the front lawn.

Wagner and Moore were rolling around in the grass, in full sight of the public, kissing and hugging like two high school kids. Terry Moore went on to be Howard Hughes' secret lover, perhaps wife, and hinted after the billionaire's death there may have been children. Robert Wagner hooked up with Natalie Wood and went through her mysterious death but never seems to have done an interview about it. However, on the parsonage set it was all business.

Robert Webb, director of the "12-Mile Reef," whom I had met at the parsonage, was looking for extras for a scene where Gilbert Roland is brought up with the bends. He asked me and a couple of my Navy buddies to stand on the dock and display our shock when they rushed by with Roland on a stretcher. We did, but guess we weren't horrified enough, since the scene was cut from the movie. Webb did hire me to clean up and put the parsonage back in its original condition. He paid me $84, big money in those days.

Maybe this is where my later urge to get into show business came from. I can remember going to the newsstand in Key West looking for magazines on writing for the movies and taking them to a room in the back of the church where it was quiet and I could read. The more I became enamored with the business, the more I realized that I could never be a dedicated member of the ministry. Besides, my doubts about where I stood with Christianity in general began to surface during this time.

But now the Key West experience was over and I soon received my orders to report to FASron 102 (Fleet Air Squadron) in Norfolk, Virginia. Typical Navy. After spending six months learning how to build, maintain and fire high technology underwater guided missiles, they assigned me to work cleaning the Squadron latrines. At least it put me on a level with Nick Adams and Andy Griffith in "No Time for Sergeants." Later this became one of my favorite movies and still is.

Chapter Five: Doing Time in "Shit City"

Most swabbies considered Norfolk the bottom of the barrel when it came to shore duty, but it sure beat being aboard ship. Although not that much, when you consider that everything in this town is built around the Navy. A Navy the local population seemed to dislike very much, while they didn't hesitate to take advantage of the money we spent. After my turn at cleaning toilets for a couple of months, I would soon settle into a routine as a clerk in the First Lieutenant's Office, something I requested.

Our job in the squadron was to fill the needs of each department in relation to supplies, etc., and manage the motor pool. The head of the office was, let's call him Lt. Braddock, a full lieutenant. He had flown fighter planes off aircraft carriers and had some doozy stories of near misses and full misses. He had retired, was an executive with a large retail chain, and was recalled during this Korean crisis. He was a hell of a guy to work for.

One day the skipper, Commander "Stevens," not his real name, thought it might be a boost to morale to start a squadron newspaper, gave the assignment to Braddock, who turned it over to me. It went great for several months until one day I was watching a PBM that had just landed, being unloaded. I noticed a large collection of bottles of booze coming off the plane and asked one of the guys unloading what was up. He said this plane was a regular run to Guantanamo Bay, Cuba, for the purpose of picking up cheap liquor.

Bingo! What better way to raise morale than write a story about a squadron plane that made regular runs to Gitmo to pick up booze for the troops. So I did in the next edition of the "FASron 102 Review," which was met by kudos from the non-coms and some officers, but with a withering response from the Admiral across the hanger in Fleet Air Wing 5, under which our squadron operated. He said that the article embarrassed the Wing and for that matter the entire Navy. Give me a break.

Braddock grabbed me and said the Captain ordered in no uncertain terms to retrieve every copy of the paper with the implication I was to put them where the sun doesn't shine. Quickly, I began begging for copies until I had covered every department in the squadron. I was afraid to count them because the pile didn't seem thick enough, but I assured Braddock I had rescued as many copies as possible. What really pissed me off was the fact I didn't even know about the cheap booze until that day of unloading.

I had to thank Braddock for saving my life once while I worked for him. On weekends I went to Washington, DC, where my wife was staying with her sister and brother in law until we could get a place in Norfolk. On one such weekend, I was scheduled to get a free ride to DC on a MATS (Military Air Transportation Service) plane. But Braddock had work for me to do, so I missed the plane ride and would leave later with friends by car.

Braddock would never interfere with me getting home for the weekend because he knew how important it was for me to get away from Norfolk. I used to babysit for him and one night he came home so smashed that his wife had to drive me back to the base. We left the house in their new Packard that was a classic even then, and it wasn't long before I discovered the wife had slugged a few herself and she got lost, even with sober me giving her directions she didn't follow.

But we eventually did arrive at my barracks, and although I really didn't think she was in any condition to drive home I couldn't invite her in to the barracks with a bunch of probably drunk and most certainly horny guys as a welcoming committee. I asked Braddock the next day if she got home okay, to which he replied, "Sure, why?" Officers never admit any shortcomings to non-coms. Now back to the office the day of the near-death event.

I watched the MATS plane take off out my window thinking how easy it would have been to fly to Anacostia Naval airport and my wife living close by would pick me up. I watched

20

this hulk in the sky, barely at the end of the runway, but about 300 feet airborne, shudder with no warning, turn slightly to the left and plunge to the ground where it was immediately engulfed in flames. No one survived, and it almost made me reconsider the religion business.

But my cushy job, which I had initially finagled, was soon to come to an end. After all, I was trained in underwater guided missiles and, although the Gunner in charge sat right across from me sharing our office, I had never set foot in the missile shop. Nor did I have any desire to do so. I had recently made Third-Class Petty Officer, so the Gunner decided it was time for me to work in my rate, took it up with the skipper and there was nothing Braddock could do about it.

Before my wife joined me in Norfolk, I lived in the barracks. During this time, I shared some interesting evenings with guys who were also horny and thirsty, but had the duty and couldn't leave the base. One guy from West Virginia, who would drink Listerine for its alcoholic content when he couldn't get to the real stuff, would organize PJ parties. Yes, we were saved by Jesus, and I don't mean the spiritual kind. PJ stood for "Purple Jesus," and it consisted of lots of vodka, cut with a little grape juice.

We requisitioned a new 50-gallon trashcan, in which we mixed the brew, and stirred it with a broom handle, not so new. Our PJ parties became legend around the base and soon we were taking reservations from those outside the barracks. Lifetime membership cost one-fifth of vodka. Booze was off limits in the barracks, making it necessary to hide the leftover Purple Jesus, so we enlisted the petty officer in charge to help us.

Everything went fine until we had a surprise inspection one evening by the most feared officer in the squadron. This guy would put you on report for the slightest infraction, like dust on the top of your locker, so he had a field day when he walked in on about 25 drunken sailors. Can you visualize that many guys inebriated to the gills standing around a large tin receptacle full

21

of booze dipping in regularly for a refill? Well that's what the asshole lieutenant saw.

Not only were we put on report, but we had to go before the Skipper to face charges. Luckily, he liked his booze, too, and only reprimanded each of us with an order to stay sober while in the barracks. I am sure in the back of his mind he knew we would pick up where we left off very soon with a new 50-gallon can, but with improved security on our part. The Lieutenant putting us on report didn't fare as well. Somehow he managed to fall off the ship in the middle of the night.

Part of the squadron went on board an aircraft carrier for maneuvers soon after, including our favorite officer, but also including some of the guys caught in the drink fest. I wasn't there but when they returned to the squadron, the Lieutenant wasn't with them. Seems he was lost at sea, with absolutely no witnesses. There was an investigation, but with no one available to testify to what they saw that night, the matter was finally closed.

On another occasion, this time hitching a ride to Washington with a Navy Chief Petty Officer and one other guy I didn't know, we were sailing up U.S. Route 1 on a rain soaked highway at speeds that wouldn't have been safe if it had been dry. And if the Chief had been sober. He got too close to the car in front and had to swerve into oncoming traffic where we collided head-on with another car. Of course there were no seat belts then, and the front seat passenger was definitely in harm's way.

The collision caused us to start rolling over several times, throwing me through the front windshield in the process, which turned out to be a blessing. I ended up with several bad scratches along my arms and face where I exited through the glass, but the kid in the back was crushed and eventually died. The inebriated Chief was unscathed. As they do today, the Navy takes care of its own, and I am pretty sure the drunken Chief did not suffer that much for the death of this young sailor.

When I was thrown from the car window, it took what seemed like an eternity to hit the ground. I could hear the car crashing over and over, and I was thinking, am I going to fall in its path? I didn't, but then was immediately horrified to see that the front of the car we hit wasn't there. I rushed over to see if I could help, and found a young child screaming and straddling part of the engine, which was in the front seat. The parents were unconscious. Whisked off to emergency, I have no idea what happened to this family.

Chapter Six: The Rush to Discharge

My boss, a full lieutenant, would make periodic trips to Anacostia Air Station in Virginia just outside D.C. and not far from where my wife and daughter were living with her sister. I would fly with him there, as I did on other occasions when he was checking himself out for certain weather certificates. We were on our way to Anacostia one evening with the Lieutenant in the back seat, and me in the front of the SNJ trainer. It was already dark and about halfway to D.C. he lost the lights in his cockpit.

We were using the radio beacon for navigation, so it was relatively easy for me to take over flying the aircraft, since he had given me some basic instructions in the past. At least that's what we thought. Just before entering the approach to Anacostia, we lost the radio beacon, and due to my inexperience we veered off course and ended up in Pentagon air space. We were immediately welcomed by four military jets that escorted us down, with one on each side. Nothing like an official welcome to the U.S. Capital.

Eventually my wife moved to Norfolk into Navy housing where there was another Navy couple next door with home we became close friends. They knew the best places in Norfolk to have fun and one weekend took us to one of their favorite drinking haunts, Baxter's Barn. It was just that, a barn, but there was a great Country and Western band and hundreds of gallons of beer, mostly served in pitchers. This, and another similar kind of situation in Des Moines, shows my ambidexterity for consuming any kind of booze.

One night on the way home, while riding in the backseat, I tried to crawl out the window, going at least fifty miles an hour. To this day I have no idea what I was trying to get to or from, although the next day my friend told me I kept saying "take me home." Sounds like good lyrics for a country song? The one key thing I remember about Baxter's Barn was the girls serving the beer. In short shorts, they were all a forty-four-plus and their country-style shirts were unbuttoned down to the navel.

From big boobs to drunk sailors, I finally got out of the guided missile shop by volunteering for Shore Patrol. No one in their right mind in the service volunteered for anything, but I was desperate. I had three months to go before discharge, and as an SP, much of my time was spent hauling drunken sailors off Norfolk's Granby Street and returning them to their ships. That alone should have toned down my drinking because when a sailor gets drunk, there has been no comparison I have ever run into since.

On one patrol my partner, who was about my size, and I were pulling this hulk of a swabbie up the gangplank of a destroyer when all of a sudden he bolted and fell over the side into the water. The Officer of the Deck was an Ensign who said to leave him there because they had something to help fish him out. Apparently, he did this every time he went ashore. As we were leaving, someone had moved a hoist to that side of the ship and the swimmer was being brought aboard.

Norfolk became very boring after moving out of the barracks, except for one incident with my brother-in-law. He and his wife lived out of town, but were paying us a visit on this particular occasion. He liked to drink as much as I did, and his wife always accused me of leading him astray, with which my wife usually agreed. It was an albatross I would carry with me for years that didn't even slow down my imbibing habits.

I cannot count the number of bad influences I am supposedly guilty of, but I know deep down in my liver that they all were adults, of a sound mind—at least most of them—with the ability to make decisions on their own. But I carried the mantle with enthusiasm and in most cases, with pride. Although I have to admit that in several instances I was the first to shout, "It's time for a drink." That was like a call to action for me that had become the most important thing in my life.

So, in spite of the reluctance of his wife and mine, the two of us innocently announced that we were going out for haircuts. Reluctance, most likely due to the fact that both of us had recently had our haircut. We persisted, and headed out to a bar I had frequented during my barracks days close to Virginia Beach. The Navy, and certain ladies looking for sailors, hung out here in large numbers.

Within a short time we were both on our way, and my brother-in-law insisted on buying a round for all the swabbies in the bar. That resulted in several of them buying us a drink, and this led to oblivion on my part. I woke up a couple of hours later in a booth with two other drunken guys, neither of which knew each other nor me. They had no idea what happened to my brother-in-law. But the bartender said he watched him leave and he was in no shape to get too far.

My first reaction was that he must have gone home, although I didn't think he would just desert me in the bar if he had. I was right, as I would find out later, after suffering the wrath of two furious women. I meekly suggested that we immediately head to Virginia Beach to look for the lost one. I knew he wouldn't have been able to get too far in his shape but did not tell them just how drunk he was. Since it was already late, we were soon forced to give up the search. I didn't sleep in my bed that night.

At the insistence of my wife, I headed out early the next morning looking for the guy, whom I hoped had found a safe place to spend the night. He must have, since when I found him everything seemed perfectly fine. He had apparently made two new friends and was still half-smashed and swore he could not remember anything about the night before. I took him home to his wife, who, along with my wife, pampered him. Both looked at me with complete disdain.

I find it interesting how some guys know just how much to drink when they are out trolling the bars and know when to stop, or at least slow down, when they meet someone interesting for the evening. If they are on the prowl they instinctively realize they are about to score, and drinking into unconsciousness will not get the job done. I, on the other hand, seemed to relish my find so much that I had to celebrate it with more booze. Even if we made it back to my room it was usually lights out pretty quick.

On the other hand, the same gents who know how to curb their drinks when they are out roaming can spot a drunk female in a minute and stay away. Not me. My pastoral background taught me to be a good listener, regardless. Of course three martinis helped, at least as far as the listening was concerned. But it played hell with being able to score after taking the time to listen to an impassioned life story from someone you don't know and will never see again.

I would compare my discharge from the Navy with the day several years later when I would find out I didn't have prostate cancer after switched biopsy records had proven the diagnosis wrong. Relief with a capital "R." The incident almost resurrected my boozing habits after years of sobriety. And I cannot recall any other occasion that brought me this close to the bottle, but I can say that during this one time and in every other instance my wife, Barbara, was there as my support.

But discharge happened and none too soon. My last fling at Navy authority landed me on report when I told a Chief Petty Officer, another service recall, in the guided missile shop that I didn't understand why I couldn't stay on shore patrol until my discharge three weeks away. I found out the reason: 10,000 very small weapon parts needed dusting. Because I had questioned his authority, I had to remove each of the 10,000 items from the bin that housed them, dust them, and return them to their proper place.

The petty officer in charge of the inventory was instructed to observe me closely to make sure I did what I had been ordered. Since I thought this was completely chicken-shit and was solely because I was on my way out, I decided to be a good boy and do just as I was told. Having been another of those recalled to duty for the Korean conflict himself, my overseer also thought the whole thing was chicken shit, and just ignored me. He did tell me just how close I had come to a courts marshal.

Although the missile shop Chief's incident might cure the maverick in some, it only pissed me off that much more, a trait that I still retain with extreme fondness. But this characteristic would not serve me well in the immediate future while I attempted to navigate through four years of college. If any of my readers came out of the Korean War and took the GI bill to go to college, many of you must have run into the public's reaction that you were only in school for the money.

Chapter Seven: A Brief Rendezvous with Elvis

But there was one interesting moment in Norfolk that ended up looking like the Keystone Kops. A test of missile weapons was ordered, and I was selected to supervise the maneuver. I boarded the small vessel early in the morning and we pushed off and traveled several miles off the Norfolk coastline to a buoy that housed the electronic signal—representing a ship's rudder—that would attract the guided torpedo; we also called them a fish. My first job was to confirm the buoy was functioning, which I did.

The weapon—with a homing device tuned to the buoy's signal—would launch from a submarine that was a few miles away. Traveling from there, the plan was for the missile to strike the buoy, exploding a small warhead that would prove the feasibility of our fish. Following the launch, I was basically in control of the ship, because only I knew the mechanics of how the torpedo would perform. In the Navy, and probably other services, it was extremely tough for an officer to give up command to enlisted personnel.

The vessel's skipper, a Lieutenant, Jr. Grade, knew that I was supposed to take over following the launch, but I could tell he was cocky with his new command and might not follow standard operating procedures. I was right. No sooner had they launched the missile, and through my binoculars, I spotted and announced the torpedo's wake on the way to the buoy; the Lieutenant ordered our engines to start. He wanted to get a closer look, even though he had been instructed that it could engage the live missile.

He had been briefed to shut down the engines prior to the launch to avoid attracting the fish to the motion of our rudder. I literally ordered him to cut power, and he looked at me with the disdain of an officer to an enlisted man, ignoring my order. I took another look, and the torpedo had done an abrupt turn and was headed straight for our stern, and, therefore, the rudder. By now, the Lieutenant was viewing this through his own binoculars, and I saw him mouth "holy shit."

He finally ordered the engines shut down, and the missile again turned toward the buoy. The physics of this was that we were closer to the launch site than the buoy, therefore, it was natural for the fish to home in on us until the buoy became the predominant signal. I was watching intently when I heard our engines start again, with the torpedo immediately making another turn toward us. The Lieutenant thought we were finally out of range.

You won't believe this, but he did it yet one more time and as the missile was making its way toward us, I saw it go dead in the water. It had used up its battery life, which had run out of power because of Captain Queeg's hilarious but dangerous shenanigans. Now…I had to get in the water and straddle the weapon that had surfaced by now, and disarm the warhead. Not terribly dangerous, but unnecessary, and it meant the mission had to be scrubbed.

I let the Lieutenant know that my having to abort the mission would be written up in my report just as it had happened. I think he knew what was going to happen: he lost his command.

Later, the only thing I regretted about returning home was leaving the Baxter's Barn friends. My drinking buddy was a career sailor from North Carolina, but there would be a reunion for us in the future. In the meantime, we left "shit city," as it was known to the swabbies. A reason for this was that Norfolk residents placed signs on their lawns that said, "dogs and sailors stay off the grass." Some guys worried over this but my take was, once finished with my tour here, I would leave Norfolk and probably never return.

We headed home to what we knew, Jackson, Tennessee.

I realized it the minute we got there; just didn't feel right knowing I might spend the rest of my life in Jackson, Tennessee. High school had been fun, and although we still had the same friends there, the restlessness returned. But I tried applying for and landed a job at the only local TV station as a director and all-around production person because of my experience as photographer with the local newspaper. This was when people were making names for themselves in this business, and I wanted a part of the action.

It was 1954 and television was in its infancy. But even the thought of an offer for a country boy like me to get into a glamorous business like this still didn't feel right, that is, if I had to do it in Jackson. I decided if I could do it in there, I could do it in Memphis, and at the same time attend Memphis State (later to become University of Memphis) on the G.I. Bill. In those days educational institutions, at least Memphis State, looked on the GI Bill with skepticism as if we were in it just for the money.

Taking five classes a semester, I knew it would be tough to handle with work, too, but I felt invincible at that age. Sometimes I would get so far behind I would stay up all night to catch up. Once when I requested the Dean let me drop two classes—after the final drop date—because I had gotten so far behind, he said, no, and added, "Dunning, I know why you are here (the money) and you'll never graduate." When he handed me my diploma on graduation day, I looked him right in the eye but didn't shake his hand.

And believe me, the two-hundred-sixty-dollars per month, even then, would not support most families. I worked nights until graduation and survived on "thrill pills" to keep me awake and a one-hundred milligram vitamin B1 for energy. The thrill pills were actually diet suppressants, so I saved money on food. And I only fell asleep once, in William Spenser, which was a requirement of my English degree. Although I was treated as a step-student, the University of Memphis doesn't hesitate to ask me for money now.

As a smaller fish in a larger market, I was offered a job at WMC-TV, Channel 5 in Memphis, but would have to start as a studio cameraman, and because of my experience in photography, also as a nighttime newsreel photographer. While in school, it was necessary to put the heavy drinking on hold, but spending the day in classes and the evenings working and studying left no time anyway. This random discipline in abstinence would come in handy when I finally decided to give up the drinking life.

This was only momentary until one night a couple of guys from the station talked me into going out and having a few drinks at an after-hours place. Fortunately, it was Friday and no school the next day, so there was no reason to curb my intake, resorting to the old habits of drinking until I couldn't move. My friends brought me home to a very unhappy wife who left me at the front door in a lump. Somehow I managed the control to not do that again for a while.

Eventually I left this station to work for a competitor in Memphis, and for more money. However, Channel 5 did have its moments, one of which turned out to be a very famous one, at least as the future would dictate. I met a very young, and still on the way up, Elvis Presley, one night. He just walked into the studio and said hello. He had asked the receptionist if he could see the studio, the door was open and we weren't on the air, so he caught me in the middle of setting up the next show.

He very politely asked if I would give him a tour of our studios, which I readily agreed to. By this time the engineering crew was congregated around the window from the control room to the studio trying to get a good look at Elvis. Actually, I was embarrassed, since our main studio where we were at the time was converted from the offices of an old bank building and looked like it. Since this was my first job in television and these were the pioneer years, the 1950s, we were just beginning to make the rules.

I showed him around, explaining that almost everything live he saw on the tube from this station came from this studio. There was also an announcer's booth, a small cooking show studio downstairs, and a stage on the second floor with an auditorium for special events. But we still did the bulk of our "productions" from this area that was not much bigger than a large living room. Hey, this was the beginning of TV, where it all started.

But Elvis seemed impressed, and, that said, I still cannot tell you just how much fun I had in this oversized playroom, because we were just learning what television was all about and still setting the guidelines. Guidelines we changed on a daily basis to make things more entertaining for the public. This often included mistakes that completely broke up the crew, but as the guy in charge, I had to remain cool in the chaos. However, there were a couple of times when it was so bizarre that I almost lost it.

Before the King left the studio, he reached into his pants pocket and pulled out a Zippo lighter and showed it to me. He asked me if I thought something like this would sell with his picture on it. It was Colonel Parker's idea, he told me. I replied that I was sure anything with *his* picture on it would sell. He thanked me for everything and even graciously waved to the control room crew before leaving. I had taken him in to meet them and he was fascinated over how we produced shows.

It wasn't until later I realized that at this point he had not yet appeared on the "Ed Sullivan Show." That was September 9, 1956, when 60 million viewers watched the birth of the "King of Rock and Roll." Elvis garnered a whopping 82 percent of the television viewing audience. If he had been on the "Ed Sullivan Show" before coming into our studios, I'm sure it would have been a huge let down. But he did leave appreciative, and the next time I saw Elvis Presley was on the "Really Big Shew."

Chapter Eight: The Early Days of Television

We arrived in Tennessee in September of 1994, just in time for the fall quarter at Memphis State in Memphis, later to become the University of Memphis. Colleges and universities across the country were being besieged by veterans chomping at the bit to take advantage of the GI Bill for education. Some were serious, but others just wanted the monthly paycheck. I was in the former, but I still needed the paycheck. Now, we are talking the late 1950s, and the minimum wage was one dollar.

I had to supplement the government check of around $260, and my first job in Memphis was at the Black & White store, where I tried but failed to sell clothing to low income people. I never figured out exactly, nor were any of the people I worked with or for, able to tell me just what the store name stood for. I was still somewhat naïve, but this was the 1950s, in the South. I'll get into the race issue later in this book during a period when it wasn't wise to support integration.

I finally gave up and started looking around for something else when my wife reminded me of how I had landed a job in television in Jackson; why not here? Television was in its infancy, still black and white like the job I had just left, and still looked really glamorous to a country boy from Tennessee. After one interview I got the job as a studio cameraman and nighttime newsreel photographer at WMCT, Channel 5. Would you believe, for news film I used a small hand-carried Bell & Howell 16mm camera?

The main studio, and that is definitely stretching the term by today's standards, was a space about the size of a large living room with two cameras, a couple of monitors, and a boom microphone crammed in. Overhead was a string of Kliegl lights that lit the studio sets in use, as well as raising the temperature at least twenty degrees. As I mentioned earlier, I was ashamed I had shown it to Elvis until I found out he hadn't yet appeared on the Ed Sullivan Show and didn't know the difference yet.

Channel 5's main studio consisted of a desk here and a table there, populated with a floor staff of at least three people, meaning you had to step carefully in the limited space. If you can believe it, we were able to arrange up to six on-air sets in this confined area at one time. At the end of the room was a glass partition into the control room where the production and engineering crew worked. The double glass in between provided a sound-proof environment where at least four, sometime loud, people worked.

As I watched "Saturday Night Live" in later years, I came up with the idea of doing a TV show called "Every Night Live," which is the way we did it in those days. It was before video tape was perfected, which meant we only had one chance to get it right. With thousands of viewers watching—as well as your boss, the program director—you had better know what you were doing. Unfortunately, it didn't always look that way. In later years they would make TV shows called "Bloopers," using these mistakes.

Like once when a reporter from the local newspaper— they owned the TV station—was interviewing someone that had been in the bombing of London in WWII. The reporter was a regular, and always looked like she was just one wink away from a sound sleep, and never listened to the guest's answers. After hearing the lady's experiences in the blitz, our interviewer commented, "But you came through OK and weren't killed?" Actually a question.

The interviewee who had apparently picked up on the unconsciousness of the reporter said, "Oh no, unfortunately I was." Our newspaper person said simply, "How nice," and went on to the next question. Now the control room was on the floor with laughter and the camera crew was barely able to keep the cameras steady. I almost lost it myself, but someone had to hold the whole thing together. The strange thing was nobody but this bunch seemed to notice, indicating the popularity of the show.

The wrestling matches were in their glory during this period, and I worked camera, eventually directing the show. Our cameras were in the balcony of the auditorium where the matches were held, and had to be carefully attached to the protective railing. Advice given to all cameramen in setting up was, "if you accidentally drop the camera during setup, you might as well go over the side with it."

Now…if I told you that wrestlers' falls were pre-staged, would you believe me?

The television business was fun and exciting in those days, and my kids enjoyed it too, since I used them in commercials—unpaid, unfortunately—and you never knew what might happen. The Elvis Presley incident mentioned earlier was one of those unexpected perks of the business. However, my kids didn't speak to me for weeks after this happened because I had forgotten to get the star's autograph. Over the years I would have the opportunity to work with several stars, most of which were pleasant, some not.

It was college classes beginning at 8 AM, then rush to work at 3:30, where I would do several live shows and commercials and network station breaks throughout the evening. I had to study sometime, and that could only be done between these live shows and network station breaks, plus a couple of hours when I got home around 1:30 AM after signing off the station. Sleep was sparse and I survived off diet pills to keep me awake and vitamin B1 for energy. You repeated this from earlier.

One night it all came to a head when there was complete chaos in the control room. All of a sudden during a live show that I was directing, I found myself standing on the console that housed all the control monitors and the goose-necked mike I used to communicate with the studio crew. I was screaming instructions incoherently into the microphone, with everyone around me completely startled over what was happening. The engineer who sat next to me finally got me down off the ceiling.

One of the studio crew came in and took over the show. The pressure of school, live TV and no sleep, along with the diet pills that nearly drove me off the edge by themselves, had been too much. At the hospital later it was determined that I had a pre-ulcer condition that could become full blown if I didn't slow down I did...well, maybe, just a little bit. The introduction of video tape made everything much easier, since all that was necessary with the new technology was, do it over.

I moved from Channel 5 to Channel 3, WREC, eventually to become WREG-TV, when purchased by *Look Magazine*, then the *New York Times* from the previous owner who was an eccentric with idiosyncrasies you wouldn't believe. My father went to Mississippi State with him, where he had a real quirky nickname, "Noisy". But it was his kind of entrepreneurship in the early days of television that made it the great industry it is. Today, most of television, except the creative, is controlled by computers.

The station owner had a huge house set back almost a half mile off the highway that led into Mississippi from Memphis. He had one of the best stereo sound systems in the country, and neighbors would comment they could hear music coming from his house at night from as far away as a half-mile. I once drove by there just to see if it was true and noticed several people parked on the side of the road listening to the music. I once made the comment that he should sell tickets.

These were the days when everyone was building bomb shelters and this guy had the very best, completely stocked and outfitted to house everyone in his family. It was a trait he carried out in the business as well by hiring several members of his family as key personnel at the station. However, when his sister was asked once if having the bomb shelter available made her feel secure, she replied, "I'd rather take my chances with the bomb."

When the studios were being renovated from just radio to include television, the station owner showed up one day during construction. He observed for a while, then, introducing himself to the workers, he proceeded to instruct them that all the grooves in the screws on the moldings were to be vertical so they wouldn't collect dust. And, once I missed an unscheduled station break, and he had me on the phone in less than a minute. I told him I had to go to the restroom. He told me to learn to regulate myself.

Chapter Nine: The Peabody Hotel Ducks

WMC-TV was downtown on one of the major streets of Memphis in an old building across the street from a Krystal Burger. It was a quick meal, and the staff at Channel 5 ate there often. We referred to their small, square sandwiches as BO burgers due to the smell. But they were delicious, if you could just hold your breath. Our regular waitress was Nell and she wasn't in the least impressed with celebrities, especially those behind the camera. Nell taught me, if you get bad service somewhere leave a penny tip.

Krystal Burgers was the equivalent of the Midwestern chain, White Castle, and opened its first location in Chattanooga, Tennessee, in 1932, where you could buy six Krystals and coffee for 35 cents. The reason I bring all this up is that it was the White Castle in Des Moines where I labored over these delicacies to try and sober up before going home. Most of the time, I heaved them in the bushes at my front door. But it was amazing how the plants in that location thrived over the others.

Eventually I moved over to WREC-TV (later to become WREG), Channel 3, with studios in the basement of the Peabody Hotel. The Peabody had its own stories. It was, and still is, famous for its ducks that swim in the fountain in the hotel lobby. Every evening they are put to bed by their caretaker by rolling out a red carpet that stretches from the fountain to the elevator bank. Apparently this feature brought in visitors from all over the world, some not so good for these innocent fowl, as you will see.

The ducks are marched into the elevator on the carpet and taken to the roof where their penthouse was located. No one but the caretaker is allowed to ride with the ducks. The next morning the procedure is reversed and the ducks are returned to the fountain through the elevator, via the red carpet to the fountain. You are allowed to stand around and observe but you can't get too close to the ducks. Unfortunately, this kind of protection would prove inadequate in a mindless display of stupidity.

The hotel was hosting a group on one occasion, which I believe was a bunch of college fraternity alumni; my memory is vague, since this has been almost fifty years ago. The Peabody had a mezzanine that surrounded and looked over the lobby, and a cluster of the frat guys had congregated around the mezzanine with drinks in hand. The ducks were still innocently swimming in the fountain entertaining the guests. As usual, there were several people standing around the fountain looking at the ducks.

All of a sudden, a barrage of drink glasses began to hit the fountain and some of the ducks, even guests. They were coming from the drunks on the mezzanine, and the volley went on for several minutes until security stepped in to stop the chaos. My recollection is that some ducks might have been killed, others injured. No guests were hurt. The frat guys were questioned but no one would give up the culprits. In my lifetime I have been on many drunken tears but would never do something like this.

We had out-of-town friends visit us regularly in Memphis, but our favorites were
"Warren" and "Jessica," not their real names, from Norfolk, while in the Navy. (Remember Baxter's Barn?) They wanted to go to the Peabody and see the ducks, then go to the roof where there was dancing. We were too late to see the ducks this particular night so we proceeded upstairs where the band was already playing. The Peabody roof bands were featured regularly on CBS radio nationwide.

A friend of mine who had one of the finest radio voices I had ever worked with, "Harry Rhodes," not his real name, was doing a band broadcast on the network that night. Harry rarely committed a blooper, but this night he was somehow rattled when introducing the show and said, "And now CBS presents the music of Benny Firestone coming from high atop the Potel Hebody." He repeated that three more times before getting it right. The drunks didn't know the difference.

Harry was otherwise flawless during our visit, and we all danced until after midnight, then decided to take a walk around the roof. A mistake. Jessica and I made up our minds we would climb up on the wall that was designed to keep people from going over the edge, with a wrought iron extension. Out of sight of security, we walked the edge until we were behind the bandstand looking for who knows what. When you're smashed, the only reason you need to do something is that you want to do it.

All of a sudden, we found ourselves in front of the ducks' penthouse. How they could sleep with all the music and other noise going on at the dance floor was hard to understand, but they did seem to be sleeping. That is, until Jessica awakened the ducks and sat down on the concrete roof to hold about a fifteen-minute conversation with them. At times it almost looked like they understood her, and I am reasonably sure that she at least thought she understood their quacking.

WREC-TV, which later became WREG, was in the basement of the Peabody, right next to the men's restroom. Don't know if there was a discount for this location, but radio had been there for years and the space was simply expanded to include television. I moved there from Channel 5 for more money, which seemed reasonable at the time, but little did I know the move would be the stepping-stone to launching one of my most heavy drinking periods.

It was here that I toyed with the idea of moving to a TV network job in New York as an assistant director. It was a job that included making network breaks, getting coffee for people that mattered, and staying out of trouble. One of my colleagues at WMC-TV had taken this road and eventually ended up directing the "Ed Sullivan Show." I was ambitious and felt confident I could do as well but I was, after all, a country boy. And there was a big family to consider.

I talked to my wife and we discussed the impact on our three kids, but equally the huge difference in the cost of living. There was never really a doubt that big sacrifices would have to be made in our standard of living, which would curtail a lot of things we did in Memphis and took for granted. All things considered, we decided not to make the move; it was cinched when I found out how much it cost to drink in New York. In later years traveling there it made no difference, since I was on an expense account.

Afterwards, when I had decided to get out of the TV business, I felt even more ambitious than when I had considered going to the Big Apple working for a TV network. But what to do with a degree in English, a large family, and now a house to pay for? And then someone said to me, with your ability to bullshit and drink, get in the selling game. I started hitting the classifieds regularly and cannot tell you how many fruitless interviews I went on.

It was only by chance that I followed up on an ad from a company in Des Moines, Iowa, for a salesman to sell a line of lifestyle books in a new territory being established in Memphis. It covered five-and-one-half southeastern states, and I figured as long as I wasn't going to have to live in Des Moines, it was OK. But I also felt sure this amount of geography would mean a high paying job with lots of amenities and perks. Little did I know I was wrong, on all counts.

One, I would eventually end up living in Des Moines and two, the position paid barely more than the paltry sum I was making in television. The only perk was an expense account. I would eventually learn from more seasoned salesmen that when you turned in your expense account each week, you had just written a piece of fiction. Little did I know that my fiction-writing career would start as a sideline to selling books. But I must admit that there is an art to this kind of "corporate bonus."

The sales manager of this company came to Memphis to interview me, and he stayed at the Peabody Hotel where I worked in the basement for the TV station. I had to get into the hotel and up to his room without anyone seeing me. It took some finagling, but I was able to get away without anyone knowing what I was doing. He was a great guy and we hit it off immediately, and I was asked to come to Des Moines for another interview. In those days, most of the planes landing there were DC-3s.

The minute I got off the airplane in this cold, desolate looking place I reached the conclusion that I didn't want to be in Des Moines, Iowa. I was brought up in the South where the weather could be challenging, but I would rather spend the rest of my life in Jackson, Tennessèe, than one day in Des Moines. I would also come to understand a saying passed around by this company's alumni: "It's a nice place to work if your family can afford to send you."

It was winter, very late, and I got a real solid clue of what to expect the minute I walked down the outside deplaning ramp and through a space recently cleared for passengers. It led through a typical very dirty snow to the terminal entrance. A cab took me to a motel, almost next door to the airport that looked like what the Holiday Inn was trying to replace. There was no restaurant and I had not had dinner, so I was forced to dine on two candy bars and a bag of peanuts. I could hardly wait for the next day.

I made the rounds of just about everyone that mattered, and ended up with the guy I would be working for and drinking with for several years to come. We hit it off right away and went to lunch together, in the company cafeteria. The food wasn't bad, and there were several people there that I would realize later that preferred the iced tea lunches rather than the two martini ones. But little did I know this lunch was a move to keep me sober for the big cheese whom I would meet that evening.

Chapter Ten: Even Worse Than "Shit City"

The dinner would end up being legend…at least for me. The storied part was my official introduction to the martini, which is basically when I felt I formally donned the lampshade. I was on my second drink before dinner when they made me an offer of a job, including salary. I knew I had come in there with two guys, but right now there were four at the table with me. It was then that I excused myself to go to the restroom. After almost colliding with a waiter preparing a Caesar salad, I finally made it.

I didn't really have to go, but needed the time in a stall with a piece of toilet paper and my handy pen to calculate whether or not they were offering me more money to take this job than I was already making. Try to calculate numbers after two martinis and no food and write results legibly. It took a while, but I finally decided the offer was OK, although this was not confirmed until I pulled out the piece of toilet tissue the next day and deciphered what looked like Egyptian hieroglyphs.

In my half-smashed state I finally decided to take the job despite the fact the salary was only a few bucks over what I was already making. It was the future, my roiling gut was telling me, only to learn later, that, too, was a dream. I did it, in part, because I fell in love with the martini and was convinced that this job was the launching platform from where I could best develop the habit. I would learn that this assumption was correct. Although a very dumb reason, at the time it made perfect sense to me.

Even though I had to lower my salary expectations, but because I learned to cherish martinis while being interviewed in Des Moines, it would have been just wrong not to extend this potential business skill. I felt it only natural to parlay this new-found agent of proselytization into the beginning of a new selling career. The two-martini lunch, which often extended way beyond that, lasted for all the years I was in sales and well into the 1970s. Many of us mourned over its demise.

44

What better way was there to convince a client that he wanted what you had to sell than by pouring a couple of martinis down him, then getting his name on the dotted line? I am overemphasizing, sorta, the booze part, but I can tell you, it did help to loosen everyone up and reduce some obstacles. It is not, however, a panacea for good preparation and knowledge of the product. Those days are over, but many of us will always remember the two-martini lunch as legend in the late 1950s and into the 1960s.

So I took the job, returned to Memphis, and prepared to cover five and one-half Southeastern states in a brand new 1960 Chevrolet Impala the company bought for me, another dividend paralleling the expense account. One that I would eventually trash on a side street in Mobile, Alabama. I wasn't drinking or even hung over. Just preoccupied with a new job and somewhat overwhelmed with the amount of geography to cover. For the record, there were 259,483 square miles in this conglomeration of states.

To start with, the guy who hired me came to Memphis to break me in. He thought New Orleans would be a good place to start. Louisiana, along with Tennessee, Arkansas, Mississippi, Alabama and the panhandle of Florida were included in my province. Once I had spent two days there with the boss, in only one night it was obvious why he had picked the "Big Easy." I have never gotten over Bourbon Street, but there is nothing easy about drinking your way through New Orleans. Fun, yes. Easy, no.

The boss returned to Des Moines on a flight out of New Orleans and at the time, I wondered if he had made a huge mistake in hiring me. We got lots of work done, while at the same time taking in a gigantic amount of booze. I continued my trek across the Gulf Coast and into Pensacola where I added another serious drinking buddy to my growing list. He was my local book distributor, and he loved Scotch, something else I had developed a taste for back in my television days in Memphis.

My new client, and long-time friend-to-be, invited me to his home for dinner, an event that played out on every subsequent trip I made to Pensacola. I soon found that all it took to keep this man happy—and loyally pushing my books—was to bring a bottle of good Scotch for dinner, which we both proceeded to finish during the evening. In the backyard, where his most gracious wife would serve us dinner. It was hard for me to figure out if it was the liquor or just the comradery.

One night we didn't make it back into the house—couldn't actually—for coffee after dinner, and his wife left us to sleep in the backyard on two lawn chairs. Waking up to a Florida sun in your face with a monumental hang over is something not to be desired. Add to that, a barrage of mosquitoes that were apparently attracted to the Scotch taking flight from my pores, and you have in this case a comical but aggravating situation. I could never tell if the wife's reason for leaving us there was just convenience or reprisal.

Next, there was Shreveport, in the northwestern part of Louisiana with Bossier City its neighbor and in those days wide open for gambling and all kinds of nightlife. I didn't gamble much but I did drink a lot. There was a place by the name of Mothas—think I have the name right—in Bossier city that served good, reasonable drinks and all the bartenders were young gals, well endowed, and good looking. Don't remember how I found the place but it soon became my home away from home while there.

You always got the feeling you were going to score, whether you did or not, so needless to say, I consumed a lot of Scotch in this joint. My rationale was still to drink it up, celebrating a potential prize that never happened because I drank it up too much. Jeanie was my favorite server at the bar, and she regularly tried her best to slow down my consumption of drinks. Didn't work. To this day I do not know if she would have responded to my advances should I have ever been able to make one.

I was fast honing my doctrine of "Let's hurry up and get drunk." That in itself was an obstacle to making out and a definite hindrance to finding your way back to your motel room if you did. But if you were lucky on both counts, the outcome was still likely to be a bust. Now, why do you suppose a guy who got an erection when he walked onto an airplane to travel would spend serious time courting a young lady only to fizzle out in the process plastered? Booze and amour just don't mix.

And this is a good time to discuss my carousing, which I have described here with drinking while on the road traveling, in spite of the fact that I had a wife and three kids at home. It was just more of the restlessness that has plagued me throughout my life, and which had repeatedly gotten me into trouble. I have often thought I must have had a latent guilt complex that surfaced the minute I started drinking. Eventually it got me a divorce. My first wife was better off without me and in the end came to learn this.

With all this territory to cover, I began to develop a very dangerous habit in the world of imbibing. I began to drink alone. After a full day of calling on book clients with a considerable amount of stress and driving in between, I finally settled in a motel in a new location in preparation for another day of calls. Although I was sometime dead-tired, most of the time there was always a willingness to party. But, unfortunately, in some places there was just no place to do that.

It was true of Fort Smith, Arkansas; Chattanooga, Tennessee; Monroe, Louisiana; even Jackson, Mississippi; although there were hot spots in that state where you could not only drink all night but gamble like you were in Las Vegas. Too rich for my meager salary and expense account, so in these burgs I simply returned to my room and proceeded to drink, sometime even skipping dinner. Needless to say, not only was I bored, but also malnourished.

Because of my background in television, I had contacts in Birmingham, Alabama, in the business that had moved from Memphis. Now Birmingham is certainly not my idea of a real fun town, but with willing accomplices it's easier to bring out the best or…worst. There was one guy always ready to help make it an evening of excessive imbibing, and another, a female personality at the same TV station where he worked, who decided to join us on one occasion. It was a train wreck with no destination from the first drink.

It all came to a precipitous end when we found ourselves back at my motel bar having one last drink. Just what we needed. It was obvious no one was in any shape to drive, so we headed back to my room. The guy crawled onto the regular-sized bed with the gal quickly following him. I gave it a few minutes to make sure I wouldn't interrupt what I thought was the inevitable. I was wrong. Within minutes they were both sound asleep so I joined them. We all slept until 4AM, when we seemed to come alive at once.

I had an early appointment, my male friend had an early show to do, and our female companion just wanted to know what had happened after we all hit the bed together. Since everyone was still fully clothed, she finally accepted it as an innocent, ensemble nap between three people who had, at least in this situation, decided not to drive when drunk. The real problem was when my friend showed up at his home he was confronted by a distressed wife that never spoke to me again.

Chapter Eleven: On the Road Again

In the 1960s, the bars in New Orleans stayed open 23 hours a day, required only to close for one hour to clean up. I can remember one time I was too drunk to leave and a friendly bartender let them just clean around me. One morning after spending the designated time in one of my favorite places, I suddenly realized I had to appear on a WWL radio show to promote one of the company's books. Fortunately, I hadn't had time to develop a hangover. I was still drunk, but rushed back to the hotel to freshen up.

When I arrived at the station, the couple interviewing me remarked without hesitation, "You look like hell!" They were also friends. When it was finally established that I probably would not die on the air, they promised to take it easy on me. The book I was promoting was a sewing book, which I knew nothing about except for the release copy the company had provided me. After it was over the two told me it was one of the best interviews they had done lately. According to them I was very "natural."

Now, in most cases that would be considered a compliment, coming from one of the two most popular radio personalities in New Orleans, on one of the most highly rated stations in the country. I took it at that, but the incident only added to my ever-growing concern that I drank too much. Duh. Yeah, even in those days it was obvious to me that my intake of alcohol was way too much. The problem was, I headed right back to the French Quarter that night, boozing it up again.

So, there was no choice but to move on, across the Gulf Coast, and into Mobile, Alabama, then up to Montgomery and Birmingham. I completed this two-week trip by visiting Chattanooga, then Nashville, Tennessee, my second favorite drinking hole, to Bourbon Street, Printer's Alley. Up until I reached Nashville, it was dullsville in the whole state of Alabama. After I had bankrupted the relationship with my TV friend in Birmingham, any comradery after that had to be carefully planned.

Nashville's claim to fame is, of course, the Grand Ole Opry, an institution of country music I could never abide, even smashed, although I did make a concession for this at Baxter's Barn. I do like Blue Grass but can't stand that twangy crap that is still sported by some of these entertainers. If I wasn't drinking, this kind of music drove me to it. I may lose some readers, and even my current wife who still today occasionally listens to C&W radio stations—she's from Chicago—but it still annoys the hell out of me.

In those days, Printer's Alley was one of those legal/illegal drinking places famous in that part of the country, necessary to further the commerce of the state capital, which wasn't too far away. Many of the people I met there were from the North, and many of them were fascinated with the ways, particularly the talking habits, of Southerners. But so many times I observed a local resident put on a Yankee so bad it was pitiful. This was even more bizarre if the Southerner was a good-looking young lady.

Even though I enjoyed them, the two-weekers took a lot out of me and played hell with my family life. I honestly believe this had something to do with my gypsy background, where my father was moved at least once every two years by the railroad, and I was introduced to a new city and friends. I adapted easily, even enjoyed the new adventure, but was forever restless when remaining too long in one place. Some of this has mellowed as I grow older but the urge, although somewhat dormant, is still there.

Other than gypsy, these folks are called Travelers or Roaders, and from whichever group they are, there is a rich ancestry. The groups are broken down into ethnic classes including, Cale, Hungarian-Slovak, Ludar, Rom, Romnichel or Sinti Gypsy or American (Roader), English, German, Irish or Scotch Traveler. Although as far as I know, I have no Romanian blood in me, but I am still convinced of being part gypsy. As you will see in the next few paragraphs, I almost became a full-time nomad.

In Paducah, Kentucky—where Joe entered and exited my life—there was one incident that could have changed my future radically. I was six and walked to school every day, passing a wooded area on the way. One day a couple of friends and I decided to go into the trees on the way home and try some cigarettes I had lifted from my parents. Drinking at five, smoking at six. We headed into the area and after looking around, decided on a place we could smoke our cigarettes without anyone seeing us.

We were puffing away when a man dressed in very unusual attire approached us from behind some trees, and started a conversation. Eventually, he invited us to his camp, which was just beyond the clump of trees where he had emerged. As we broke through into a clearing, there were several wooden, horse-drawn wagons parked with no semblance to a pre-determined plan, nor did it look like there was any hierarchy in the arrangement. This was 1938.

They were all beautifully painted with vivid colors and creative designs that only an accomplished artist could render. There were portraits of gypsy women smoking, brightly painted panels of red, green and blue. There were some circular wagons, others in several square shapes, all colorfully decorated. We had stumbled upon a gypsy colony that, in those days, were viewed like the poor today. The man noticed my awe at the colors and illustrative paintings and singled me out to approach.

Our host's name was Gudada, who led us into the encampment, where several people were milling around, doing what looked like to be chores. He asked me if we wanted something to eat. I said yes, but the other two just started backing up. Boris went into his wagon for the food, and the minute he was out of sight, my two friends took off running. I don't really know why, but I had to stay. He brought out a hot bowl of goulash that was delicious, and I quickly scarfed it down.

My new acquaintance was middle-aged, dark skinned, with a bushy mustache and coal-black hair; he wore a bandana over his head, a bright yellow shirt over which there was a blue-grey vest. Knee-high boots that were as black as his hair completed the outfit. He looked pleased that I enjoyed the goulash, which he told me he had cooked. My mother always said that I never met a stranger, which would be disastrous these days, and could have been then if not for a turn of events.

Gudada asked me if I wanted more cigarettes, and promised me I would have all the smokes I wanted, plus other pleasures, if I would accompany him and their caravan when they left the next day. I thanked my Gypsy friend with no commitment, and went home to find my parents in the process of calling the police, who eventually contacted my school to warn them, after which they drove the gypsies out of town. My two buddies had ratted me out. Otherwise, don't really know, I might just have joined the gypsies.

The company took care of my gypsy urge after a couple of years in Memphis. My track record was good enough to move me to a larger territory: Los Angeles, which included Southern California, Arizona and Las Vegas. Putting me in Los Angeles next door to Vegas was the epitome of the country boy going to the big city. But Las Vegas isn't just a city, it is an icon of over-indulgence. And I believe it can be as exciting as New York. That is because you can find *anything* you want in Las Vegas.

As an example, my first night in Vegas I saw *Flower Drum Song* with Jack Soo, Jerry Lee Lewis in the lounge of my hotel, grabbed a late show with Bobby Darin, and won $200 at 21. Oh yes, I got a ticket from the Las Vegas police for making a U-turn when I became completely overwhelmed by the spectacular lighting on the Strip. You can take them out of the country, but you can't take the country out of them. And by the way, at least then, Las Vegas cops were some of the most courteous I had ever run into.

I would often stay up late into the morning hours at the Blackjack table, where I quickly learned drinks were complimentary for those who played in the same location for a period of time. I'm not that good at 21, so I always picked the small dollar tables. This was one of Vegas's ways of catering to the low rollers. The high rollers received comps that included free airfare to Sin City, free rooms, and many with lines of credit in the hundreds of thousands.

Needless to say, there were a multitude of ways to get into trouble in his town, and I was guilty of falling prey to a few. What was most interesting about Las Vegas was how it maintained the perpetual festival atmosphere while being all business. But not once did I see any evidence of the mob faction in Vegas, although it was in this era that it was most active and powerful. I once asked a friend who was pit boss at the now defunct Thunderbird hotel and casino about this. He simply said, "Don't go there."

Chapter Twelve: Going to the Even Bigger City

I was soon tired of the glitter and night life that I couldn't really afford, and was ready to return to Los Angeles and my then home base of the Highlander Hotel. In the shadow of the Hollywood Bowl, it was also conveniently located close to the studios for movie and TV stars to do overnighters while working on movies or shows. I regularly ran into Dinah Shore and Vince Edwards who played *Ben Casey* in the series of the same name. Based on my experience, this place should be proclaimed an historic property.

"Abe Weinstein" was the Highlander's owner, and he immediately took me under his wing with the kind of advice that he said would help me find my way around LA. At first, I thought Abe would be my mentor, but after he had given me the typical Jewish father's counsel on life in the metropolis, he promptly cut me loose. He was initially convinced I was Jewish. When I finally persuaded him I wasn't, he just said, "Well, hell, you should've been."

With significant success in my first sales call in LA, I made the decision to take the rest of the day off, and headed back to my home away from home armed with directions from my customer. You have to understand that a country boy from Jackson, Tennessee, suddenly thrown into the big city with its accompanying conveniences, like freeways, can be immediately challenging. But the directions were good and I pulled into a parking place just outside my room in the back of the motel.

The Highlander was actually a motel built in a two-story square configuration around the swimming pool with a large opening at the front and small entrances around the sides and back. On the way up to the second floor room, the pool area was clearly visible, where I could see several guests being served drinks. There was a black guy walking around among the guests passing out the toddies and making conversation with each delivery. That got my attention.

It was still early and from my vantage point overlooking the pool, there were people to meet and things to talk about. I put on some comfortable clothes and headed down, found a spot at the pool, and proceeded to look around for where those drinks were. While surveying the group, it was finally beginning to sink in that I was in La La Land in a motel just around the corner from Hollywood boulevard. It wasn't long until the booze came to me in the form of the best vodka gimlet I would ever drink.

It was delivered by "Horace," who introduced himself as the "go-to" guy at the motel for anything I wanted. *Anything.* When I tried to pay, Horace said it was on the house for his "friends." There was no doubt that I had arrived now. And I had always heard how hard it was to make friends in LA. After a lot of conversation and a couple more gimlets—he built them strong—I decided to wander down the street to Hollywood and have dinner.

I chose Diamond Jim's Steak House because it was close and had been recommended by the hotel owners. It was on the corner of Highland and Hollywood Boulevard, and I was still half smashed from Horace's gimlets. I would later learn that enjoying his drinks would be a daily occurrence and a great time to meet interesting people. It was my introduction to what to expect in tinsel town with the place a melting pot of tourists, regulars and just plain weird types. I proceeded to have another drink.

After dinner, I headed back to the motel when I noticed the lights and a crowd in front of Grauman's Chinese Theatre. Looking down, I suddenly realized I was on the Hollywood Walk of Fame, where the stars were forever immortalized, and I knew I must go see it. Even if the additional booze I had consumed in the restaurant might make it a one-eye affair. I looked around me the best I could in the condition I was in and quickly noted that I was amongst some of the weirdest people in the world.

Just follow the stars, and there it was in all its glory. Footprints and handprints in the outside entrance; Charlie

Chaplain, Harold Lloyd's glasses, Jean Harlow, Al Jolson, Deanna Durbin, Jack Benny, Barbara Stanwyck, Humphrey Bogart, Roy Rogers, John Wayne, Ava Gardner, Elizabeth Taylor, and many more have been added in later years. It's pretty awesome to know these famous celebrities were standing right here at one time, and then I got the feeling that a part of them was still there.

Later that evening in my room doing some paperwork, there was a knock on the door. It was Horace, accompanied by a beautiful Black woman, and a tray of three gimlets. After inviting them in, we all sat on the bed—there were no chairs in the room—and drank our drinks, and, curiously, talked about…nothing. A few minutes later Horace left, alone. I looked at this gorgeous gal and said, 'What am I gonna do?' Suddenly I was reminded of just what Horace's *"anything"* meant.

And then it was Saturday, and nothing to do in LA. That's a statement only a country boy come to town could make.

Another knock on the door and, of course, it was Horace. He started with a big grin on his face, which was his way of asking how I had fared, before he told me seriously that he had someone he wanted me to meet. I quickly told him the tryst he had set up the night before had not worked because I didn't believe in paying for it. Not prejudiced, which Horace knew already, just not at the point yet where I had to pay for sex. He understood, and that was my last hooker visit, compliments of Horace.

He wanted to introduce me to a writer that was a regular resident of the motel, since he knew I was in the publishing business. His name was Bill Ballinger (his real name), and he was staying in the room adjacent to the motel office. He told me Bill had written several novels, and wrote regular television scripts for shows like "Alfred Hitchcock," "Cannon," and "Ironside." Let's see…I had just arrived in town and already was about to meet a famous author.

Horace handled the ceremonies of introduction, and left the two of us to talk shop. It was instant chemistry that survived years of a close friendship that only ended when Bill died of lung cancer. I was there in the Encino hospital right to the end, and was probably the last person to go out for a pack of his beloved cigarettes because it was already decided the end was very close. It came the next day. Bill was such a special person in my life and I still regret his passing.

But the time we spent at the Highlander turned out to be a series of hilarious experiences. One in particular was a night around the pool when three high school teachers from Oklahoma were chaperoning a class trip to Hollywood. We were drinking—Bill was a drinker but not as avid as I was—with Horace supplying the gimlets as usual. The poolside was full, as it normally was, and slowly Bill and I observed the kids were thinning out to only a few, then none.

At about 9 PM the teachers were becoming very frustrated because they had had a few drinks, and were losing track of what was going on in the students' rooms. Bill and I offered to help and began to knock on doors. The kids readily opened the doors, since they were as drunk as their teachers. It was as if the kids had been waiting the whole school year just for this opportunity. Bill finally looked at me with a big grin on his face and asked tongue in cheek, "Did we do this in high school?"

We returned to the pool area to give the teachers the bad news, and found all three of them in the water…naked. Horace was doing his best to get them out, but the teachers were having none of it. Since the only option left was for Bill and I to go into action as lifeguards to assure no one drowned, we spent the next hour or so doing our duty. The balcony around the pool was crowded by voyeurs, and we did have to fight off a couple of horny guys, but the evening ended peacefully.

Not that there wasn't consternation over how many of the high school girls would show up pregnant in the next 9 months, but that wasn't really our problem. And, I often wondered if any families tried to sue the motel. At least we were able to pour the teachers into their beds unscathed, although still nude and soaking wet. We made sure the kids were at least in their own rooms and accounted for as best we could determine. I did not look forward to my two girls entering high school.

Chapter Thirteen: Finding My Writing Mentor

At last I had found my LA mentor in Bill Ballinger, who knew his way around the city as well as anyone. One of his favorite places was also Diamond Jim's. You have to understand that Hollywood Boulevard, especially this corner of Highland Avenue, exhibits a collection of the freakiest people you will find anywhere; at least it did in those days. It was nothing for someone to walk up to you and perform a complete routine for several minutes in the hopes that you might be in pictures and discover them.

One night we came home from dinner after tons of drinks, and decided to sit by the pool for a while. Horace, of course, insisted we have one more. Our host was like the typical mother pushing her food, except his specialty was booze. Mom thought you had never eaten enough and insisted you have more and looked hurt if you didn't. Horace actually had that dejected look on his face when you turned down a drink. So I never did. Obviously, Bill and I generously took care of him.

There was a lovely young lady there by the pool reading a book, introduced to us by, who else but the Big H? Her name was Angie, from St. Louis, and she worked for the mob. That's right, Angie was a high-priced hooker with a seven-year-old son in Missouri; her goal was to make enough money to retire and take her son to Oregon. It was the first time I had ever met a real prostitute and felt her plans were commendable. She didn't look like she expected Bill or me to contribute to her retirement.

One night Angie knocked on my door around 2 AM after I had already gone to bed. When opening the door it was obvious that she was extremely nervous, and quickly asked if she could come in. I immediately noticed the bruises all over the exposed parts of her body, asking "what the hell happened?" At first she was hesitant but eventually decided to trust me. You have to understand that when you work for the mob everything is a secret, especially something like this that could get them publicity.

Some guy had paid her—big time—to let him beat her with a rope, resulting in not only bruises but burns from the lashing. He was a sadist and got his jollies hurting, not just anyone, but only prostitutes. Angie said it was just part of the business and that I shouldn't worry. Since the other hooker she shared the room with was still out on a date, she asked me to put ointment on the sores. The guy had paid dearly for his sick gratification because Angie would be out of action for a few days.

I had several conversations and dinners with Angie during my stay at the Highlander, and she confided in me about life as a prostitute. Apparently her son knew nothing about what she did; he lived with his grandparents. She was moved around the country at will and when she left L.A. she was headed for Las Vegas, then Denver. She told me by staying on the move it was less likely that she would be arrested. According to what Angie described to me, the Mob had a business just like big corporations.

Just one more episode from the Highlander, involving a well-known movie star at the time. On another lazy Saturday evening, Bill and I were, as usual, by the pool having drinks. The Highlander "Master of Ceremonies" came by about 9 PM with an announcement that there was a big party going on in two rooms next to mine. It was obvious to us at poolside that there was something going on up there, but I had not yet been here long enough to actually see one of these events.

You are probably wondering by now if Horace ever goes home to spend time with his wife and kids, whom he had introduced to us one day. In this introduction it immediately became obvious how much he cared for his family and then I thought back to the night he introduced me to the good looking hooker and quickly decided it was just a part of doing business. We learned that he spent the days with them, virtually ran the motel at night, and slept very little. You could never tell it by his enthusiasm.

Well, this was another typical Hollywood party—I didn't really know this, but Bill described similar ones he had attended—with booze and women all over the place. Apparently the big difference here was the informality provided by the Highlander. Its host was a well-known character actor of American westerns. But on this evening he wasn't acting, but rather he was welcoming guests and making sure they were well taken care of. Our mode of invitation was, of course, through Horace.

And it's a good thing it was the weekend and the motel was almost empty. I found out later this was the raucous side where they put the hell-raisers, with the opposite side for the more conservative guests. Apparently my background as a real party type must have somehow preceded me at registration.

Bill and I spent the rest of the evening there, up until four the next morning, having a hell of a time. The two rooms were adjoining, and one was set up for drinks, the other to, well…do whatever came naturally. Our host was very gracious and treated us like celebrities, who Bill was, but I was made to feel like one. The party included several movie stars, many of which were there with their wives or husbands, or… That is the reason I have decided not to mention any names.

The Hollywood Roosevelt Hotel was another landmark as much as Grauman's Chinese Theatre, which was just across the street. It hosted the first Academy Awards in 1929 and was famous for guests like Clark Gable and Carole Lombard, who stayed in the penthouse suite for five dollars a night. In later years it was said to be haunted by Marilyn Monroe, Montgomery Clift and Errol Flynn. I have been there several times and it definitely reminds one of the opulence of Hollywood.

Bill was good friends with the manager of the Roosevelt's famous Tropicana Bar, and we drank there regularly, where every other drink was free, compliments of his friend and the bartenders that served us. Needless to say, I took advantage of the situation but did not exploit the generosity. Bill introduced me to several people there he knew in the movie and television business and I began to like the feeling of mingling with the Hollywood crowd.

This all eventually had to come to an end, and it was time to check out of the Highlander and prepare to bring the family West from Memphis. I was so ready. I couldn't have taken much more—nor do I think Bill could have—so we parted with a promise to never lose touch, one that both of us kept, as you will see. Horace even makes another brief appearance later in this book but his goodbye when I officially checked out of the motel was so touching I almost broke down.

Years later at the end of 1978, I was helping Bill Ballinger with publicity on his books where he was appearing on a late night radio program on KFI. I had just recently returned to L.A. from Washington, D.C., where I had spent a couple more years working in junk mail. My current wife, Barb, and I had made up our minds that we'd do anything to get back to the West Coast, so we picked up stakes and headed there, neither of us with a job. One of the first things I did was call Bill.

He had been concentrating on writing for television in the last few years. A new, younger breed of executives were taking over the business and were looking for younger writers to appeal to that coveted eighteen to twenty-five age demographic. For my money the lack of experience was obvious in some of the work in that period; shows like "You Don't Say" and "Warrior Queen." It must have all been relative, since these inept youngsters were paid high salaries.

Bill was sixty-six by then and dealing with a problem all his similar age colleagues were of convincing these kids he knew what the younger generation wanted. We discussed this the night of his radio appearance in a bar down the street from KFI. We also talked about a novel I wanted to write about the junk mail business and the secrecy of what it does with your names. He thought it was a great idea and encouraged me then and later to write it.

Bill Ballinger died on March 23, 1980 and if for no other reason, I must write that book for him.

Chapter Fourteen: Settling in La La Land

In my Southern California territory, I spent more time in San Diego than I should have. There was the Town & Country on Hotel Circle, which was my favorite place to stay. Reasonable and elegant, with a jumping nightspot just on the other side of the circle. On one trip the company asked me to check out one of the resort hotels on Mission Bay for a sales conference, so I was able to splurge for a couple of nights on the expense account.

Can't remember the name; it makes no difference, since many have changed their names anyway. It was a great place, most of the rooms on the bay, mine included. I got the business taken care of and then settled in for some fun. While I was sitting out by the water late the first day having a drink, the man from the room next door came over and introduced himself. He was there with his wife and two kids. I wasn't really looking for conversation, since I was on my second martini heading for number three.

I'll call him Stan, because I can't remember his name, but did find out they were from Wisconsin. A daughter, nineteen, and her brother, sixteen, eventually followed Stan over, introduced themselves, and it was immediately obvious to me the girl was on the make. She was attractive but not really beautiful, and probably trolling San Diego for companionship. Because she was of age, Stan didn't seem to mind. The daughter was also holding a drink, which obviously was not legal.

We talked for a while and then his wife came over, and after some more conversation, they invited me to dinner with them in the hotel restaurant. By the time we all got there, we had had several drinks, and then proceeded to have more before dinner. The 16-year-old son was the only one sober—the father had ordered drinks for his daughter—so at least he had the good sense to try to get some food down the rest of us, but it was already too late.

I do remember struggling to get back to the room, with everyone hanging on to each other, and the son leading the way.

Naturally, we had to have just one more drink, and I guess that is what turned out the lights. The next morning I woke up sprawled on the beach, outside our rooms, between Stan and his daughter. The mother and son apparently had just left us there in the sand and gone to bed. The surf was heading closer and closer and would have soaked us soon.

I thought they drank milk in Wisconsin, but these folks completely ran against the grain of the typical profile of the conservative Midwest family. Maybe they only did it on vacation, and sometimes you do have to let it all hang out. But how is it I was always attracted to this kind of group, and they to me? Pure luck? I have often wondered, though, just how much less drinking I might have done had I not had this kind of "invitation to drinkers" look on my face. But was it really my fault? Naaaaaah!

The sales conferences held by the company I worked for were legend, at least within the organization. That was the reason for my stay at the hotel, above, with the Wisconsin boozers. These conferences were held at exotic places like the Camelback Inn in Arizona, a resort whose name I can't remember in Sarasota, Florida, and Shawnee on the Delaware in the Poconos. When I was at Shawnee it was owned by Fred Waring, who would join us regularly for lunch and dinner with stories of the past.

Most everyone was a golfer but me, but at each conference I would give it a try. Shawnee was known for its golf course in the 1960s, not easy to play on, but I gave it a whirl. Glad I did on this particular occasion, when we ran into Jackie Gleason on the ninth hole having a beer. We also stopped for one, and found a table right next to his party. He had a beautiful blond with him whom I do not think was there for her golf game. She stuck to Gleason like she was appended to his arm, acknowledging no one else.

The conversation was fascinating as Gleason and his friends discussed show business, which I was still interested in from my days in television. We had only been there for a few minutes when the great one called over a waiter and said: "I'll have another Rolling Rock and a cherry coke for the little lady." She was almost six foot tall and she sported cleavage that was near perfect in my book. She sucked on a straw in the soda, which drove everyone in my party nuts.

At another sales conference, one of my first ones when still a novice at the antics of corporate practical jokes, and after a night of serious drinking and carousing, we all gathered around the meeting table for the day's session. Almost everyone had a hangover, but mine was particularly severe, something required of newbies in the organization, but which, of course, creates insatiable thirst. Fortunately, there were two large pitchers of ice water on the table; or at least I thought so.

Noticing my plight, a veteran salesman moved one of the pitchers in front of me, also offering a glass. Just what I needed, or so I thought, so I poured a full glass and took a large gulp. My eyes almost popped out of my head when swallowing, followed by a terrible urge to throw up right there on the table. Now here's a guy, only been with the company a few months, with a mouth full of straight vodka looking around the table trying to figure out who had done this.

Someone had spiked the water with a fifth of vodka. As I surveyed the group, the team was straining to keep a straight face while the division VP was opening the meeting. Because I was new, I was determined to sweat it out and not give them the satisfaction of any pleasure over my dilemma. I slowly swallowed the liquid while I called up a level of discipline I never thought I had to keep from barfing. What I didn't know at the time was that this was standard for any new member of the sales force.

Apparently the VP not only noticed my situation, but was also familiar with the pranks played by the old timers. He looked at me and said: "Dunning, I believe we can excuse you for a few minutes." Thankfully, I was able to make a hasty exit outside where I was able to fertilize a young tree, hopefully not killing it with the added vodka. When I returned to the meeting, I audited the table of conspirators again and received looks of approval, in other words I had kept my mouth shut.

I don't know if you have ever been to the Broadmoor hotel in Colorado Springs, Colorado, but if you haven't, it is a real classy place that should never host conventions of drunken salesmen. But they did, and our gang treated it like any other place we had ever been. Ground Zero to do some serious hell-raising and boozing. Along with the obligatory business, of course. Now this is a five-star resort that sits at 6,230 feet, an altitude, which in itself is taboo to heavy drinking. Didn't even slow us down.

During our stay at the Broadmoor they were required to empty their swimming pool to clean up the broken glass at the bottom. It seems that someone, blitzed out of his or her mind, decided to pepper it with used drink glasses, many of which exploded when hitting the water from probably several stories up. To the best of my knowledge the hotel never found out who the culprit was, but the event does have the earmarks of someone who was, well, a hell-raising drinker.

And then, as only our conference planners could do, they set up a sales meeting in Des Moines just before Christmas, where it experienced some of the worst snowfall the state had seen for some time. I believe it was 1965, and as each day progressed, it got worse, paralyzing the city. We were housed at the Hotel Fort Des Moines, and even some corporate members were unable to get to their homes. Thinking back now, that might have even been careful planning by top management.

The weather was so bad that the hotel was cut off from its food suppliers, who could not make it through the snow for deliveries. One evening in particular, we were forced to eat cold cuts, which somehow didn't go with Scotch. A real clown emerged in our midst, an old timer from the home office who had somehow come up with a child's suction cup rattler. Naturally, he had to attach it to his forehead, leaving it for a while. He walked around the rest of the meeting with a big red circle on his head.

They turned us loose a few days before Christmas, and said to use our company credit cards to get home any way we could. A friend of mine whose home base was Dallas—mine was still Memphis at the time—and I decided to stick together and head South. We would take a train as far as we could—drinking our way home—then when the weather was better, split for our respective destinations. The first trick was getting a cab from the hotel to the train station. The airlines were grounded.

We did finally, and after a couple hours of negotiating were able to secure two tickets in the club car on a train to St Louis. How convenient. We returned to imbibing, regularly taking advantage of the service available. After a while, we didn't care if we ever got to St. Louis, even Dallas or Memphis. It is this kind of thinking, at least on my part, that would continue to confirm that I had a problem with booze. Briefly into the trip little did we know that another state's laws would curb our fun.

I can't remember if it was Kansas or Missouri that we were in, but all of a sudden they cut off all the booze. When my friend and I reacted like a couple of "rabids," we were told the state or county we were passing through did not allow the serving of alcohol, so they were required to close the bar. As I sat there in my seat sucking on ice, hoping this would end soon, I wondered just how long I could take this life without tanking. Finally, we left the "dry" zone because they started serving again.

At last reaching St. Louis, the two of us cabbed it to the airport. We were standing at one of the airline counters trying to book flights, but the heavy snow storm further North had overloaded Lambert Field, as it was known in those days. The clerk behind the desk had a heavy Southern accent. I still had something of a drawl, but my buddy was all Yankee. All of a sudden a plan began to formulate in my mind that would get us on a plane. Looking at my friend, I said, "Let me handle this."

I turned to him and said loud enough that the airline guy could clearly hear me: "Damn, I wish I had a MoonPie and RC

Cola." The clerk whipped his head around and looked right at me: "Where did you say you were going?" The guy with me looked amazed but quickly remarked, "Why don't you tell him." I did and each of us was on our way home within the hour. Actually, I hadn't had either a Moonpie or RC for years but, luckily, I hadn't forgotten. Later I learned all the guys had made it for Christmas.

Chapter Fifteen: The Martini Still Reigns

After leaving Memphis I bought a house in Huntington Beach, one of the several beach communities in Orange County, California, and the family settled in. It was soon very obvious to me that our new home was in a pocket of conservatism, and I wondered just how the neighborhood would accept my liberal views. No problem. All they wanted to do was party, and I was designated as the organizer. I was never really certain about why this label, but think they figured the way I drank, our place was the place to be.

Everyone did their share of hosting, but everyone preferred to have the festivities at our house. It was always BYOB, and all the families chipped in on ice, mixes and food. I guess we just knew how to throw a party, since most of the time it ended well into the morning hours. Because we all had children, the older kids were enlisted as paid chaperones of the little ones at another house. Maybe planning these parties gave me the background to organize sales conferences at the publishing company.

We all drank too much but we could walk home, so there was no concern. At one particular party at our place, it was approaching three in the morning, and everything was still going strong. I had had a tough week traveling, and fell asleep sitting on a bench next to one of my neighbors. Almost as smashed as I, he was holding a conversation with me. Now you have to understand that my chatting friend was a fighter pilot in the Navy, and we all know they have senses that must be superior. Not this time.

Another neighbor came by, noticed I was fast asleep, and looked at the guy and said: "Dusty, haven't you noticed Jack isn't answering you? Don't you know he is sound asleep?" To which Dusty responded: "That's OK. I'm not talking loud." These parties were legend, and I wish I had been sober enough to remember more of the humor that was shared. What later mystified me was the fact that in those days I was satisfied drinking at home, as compared to my bar hopping in Des Moines that never included my wife.

In another of those humorous situations, I was planning to have a contractor build a patio in back just outside the family room, and asked one of our friends who worked for a concrete firm what I should do. He said that we'd get the neighborhood guys together and do it ourselves. "It's about an eight six-pack job," he exclaimed. He was right, but it wasn't without incidents. One guy had too many beers and fell face down in fresh concrete. The worst part was we let it harden too much and we almost didn't get him out.

While still living in California, my wife and I attended regular parties at Bill Ballinger's house in Hollywood, which was originally owned by Judy Canova. Bill had married right after leaving the Highlander a gal named Lucille, who was one of the sweetest people I have ever known. Lucy was from Alabama but had done a few things on her own in Hollywood before meeting Bill. She was a beautiful lady in both her looks and her inner self.

And, the new Mrs. Ballinger really knew how to throw parties. Because of my drinking habits, we were always invited to bring the kids and sleep over. Lucy could also match me drink for drink, preferably martinis, and when she had had just enough, she would grab me and we would go looking for a palm reader. She always had a new one, and they all said basically the same thing every visit, but we kept going back. To this day I do not remember any of the outcome of the readings.

Bill attracted celebrities of his own. One in particular was a maestro by the name of Felix DeCola who was an accomplished pianist. Lucy had a baby grand in the living room that she played occasionally, but when Felix attended their parties, he turned it into magic with his artistry on the keys. One of Felix's talents was having you write your name down and then creating an original song around it, complete with words and music. Not once did I ever see him falter in a performance.

There's one more story before leaving the Ballingers in Hollywood, but first some background on the master wordsmith himself who was, by the way, born in Oscaloosa, Iowa. He was a leader in the field of mystery novels, and my favorites were *Portrait in Smoke*, *The Tooth and the Nail* and *49 Days of Death*. He also participated in the spy boom, developing a character by the name of Joaquim Hawks as a CIA operative in *The Chinese Mask*.

Bill was nominated for the coveted Edgar Allen Poe Award from the Mystery Writers Association in 1960 for his television scripts, which included "Alfred Hitchcock Presents," "I, Spy," "Cannon," "M. Squad," "Ironside," "Mickey Spillane's Mike Hammer," and "Outer Limits." He was known as the kind of writer that could be depended on to produce a top-notch script on short notice, which was in demand in Hollywood in the early days of TV.

Another experience that could only happen in La La Land was a lunch that I had with Dorothy Parker, arranged by Frederick Shroyer, at the time a literary critic for the long since defunct Los Angeles Herald Examiner. Fred and I had become friends when he was the only reviewer in LA that would touch my celebrity books. Yes, they were that bad, but Fred had a soft spot for struggling publishers' reps. He was also intrigued by the bizarre stories I told about my meetings with the books' celebrity authors.

Also, he expressed a relief that we didn't have a book by Dorothy Parker, and I assured him that none was in the planning. That meant he couldn't get in trouble with his good friend if we turned out something about her like the other pedestrian stuff we had published, and he might end up having to review it. In my case, Fred was frankly over-generous. This is all a prelude to the lunch that I will treasure as long as I live, and it has nothing to do with the number or quality of the martinis.

A Dorothy Parker fan since reading about her exploits at the famous Roundtable in the Algonquin Room at the New York Hotel of the same name, with other greats like Robert Benchley,

I don't think I have looked forward to many things in my life more than I did this lunch. My wife and I were there for dinner and the feeling of greatness still permeated the room. But this day we didn't lunch in Hollywood, not even LA, but in Monterey Park, a suburb, and where Fred and Ms. Parker were living at the time.

It was a small, busy place and Fred assured me in advance they had excellent martinis. I got lost and arrived there late, and joined the other four, consisting of Shroyer, Ms. Parker and two students from Cal State Los Angeles, where Fred also taught. I excused my tardiness, joined the party and promptly ordered a martini. The conversation had somehow gotten started on the race situation, and one of the students was from the South; this was in the early 1960s.

After a few minutes Ms. Parker turned to me and asked my opinion of the racial issue, since Fred had told her, I, too, was from the South. Do you have any idea how it feels to have someone with the stature of Dorothy Parker ask your opinion on something? Anything? I would have settled for, "What do you think of the weather today?" I looked at her and saw the inquisitive mind of a highly accomplished intellectual and it scared hell out of me. Fortunately, race is a subject I never have to think twice about.

I explained growing up in the Deep South, and based on the teachings of my parents to treat people as you wanted to be treated, I assumed this meant all people, regardless of what color they were, or what church they did or didn't attend. Never did they say the intent was directed only to whites and not meant for blacks. Not that my parents weren't somewhat prejudiced; they were of the opinion Blacks had their place, not necessarily close to where ours was.

I related stories of spending weekends at the house of my Aunt and Uncle's black housekeeper in Como, Mississippi, and talked of my high regard for "Man," also black. He was the supervisor of my Uncle's two 500-acre plantations, and one day I was temporarily lost in the cotton fields simply because I couldn't keep up with Man and just sat down, exhausted. Ms. Parker seemed not just interested but fascinated. She did not say whether she had been in the South but her questions alluded to the fact she hadn't.

Both of us, on our second martini, finally got around to just what I would do about the current race dilemma, and I suddenly realized I was the central figure in this discussion, and Dorothy Parker wasn't only asking for my opinions, but now for my solution to the problem. It actually put me off guard, but my beliefs in this issue were already set in concrete, so all I had to do was to lay them on the lunch table. Although I wasn't ignoring Fred or the other guests, I was zeroed in on Dorothy Parker.

As far as I was concerned, white, black, brown, yellow or purple…they should all be treated equally. Period. Maybe too simple, but sometimes that is not only the easiest but also the best answer. The whole controversy has been sorely complicated by white people, who for some reason, have come to the conclusion that people of color are inferior to them and should be treated accordingly. Racists. And this profile is not confined to the South. I live in Arizona today and racism is rampant here.

But isn't it all just a matter of attitude? Don't tell me you can't go against your upbringing or your more bigoted peers. You have to combine what you have been taught with what you know is right. If you weren't taught what was right, hopefully you will have an awakening. You have to measure your moral integrity and make sure it is on an equal standing with the rights of others. All of a sudden, I realized I was doing all the talking, and quickly apologized for hogging the conversation.

Fred had a look on his face that told me this lunch had been so right. The two students asked Ms. Parker some questions about her writing. Later in the meal, Ms. Parker invited my wife and me over to her house to play bridge. I didn't know the card game, but made arrangements to visit her at a later date. I normally am not impressed by celebrities, since I was in contact with so many in television and publishing. But Dorothy Parker was different. She was someone that demanded your attention.

It was at a later time that Ms. Parker's husband died, and she decided to return to New York. I wanted to think that the invitation to bridge was just another way of having a meaningful discussion with someone who was open to objective debate on a number of subjects. It was an honor that she might have thought enough of me to feel this way. I will never be able to thank Fred Shroyer enough for introducing me to Dorothy Parker and setting up this legendary lunch.

I honestly believe that Ms. Parker was starved for the kind of discourse she experienced at the Algonquin Roundtable, and this was alluded to later in books about her and her "California Experience." There is no way I would consider our conversation over lunch on this level, but I like to think it was at least stimulating for her. My current wife and I were in New York in 2002 and had dinner with a show in The Algonquin Room. I am sure "Dottie," as she was known, was there in spirit.

Dorothy Parker died in New York on June 7, 1967, at the age of 73, and I am sorry that we never had the chance to have that second meeting.

Chapter Sixteen: Celebrities and Their Books

During my stay at the Highlander, I made my first call on what was then perhaps one of the most famous bookstores in the country. Pickwick Bookshop, founded by Louis Epstein in 1938, just east of Highland Avenue on Hollywood Boulevard, was legend in tinsel town. I was in awe of Epstein and throughout my career in publishing I called him Mr. E. Because of his stature in the industry. I felt it was appropriate and he got a kick from it. I actually started out feeling intimidated by the man but shouldn't have.

On that initial visit, I pitched my book line as one of the best-selling in the business. One of them at the time was only second in sales to the Bible. This had to impress even this giant of the book business. It didn't. Mr. E. responded to my sales presentation with this comment: "Your cookbooks are a lifestyle, something I call non-books." He was very cordial and strictly business but let me know that when you say books, it means the classics, not cook books.

At first I was flabbergasted, and am sure that I looked terribly nervous in Mr. E.'s tiny office upstairs that couldn't have measured more than 6 x 6 feet. I'm never claustrophobic, but I did sense the walls beginning to consume me, which I would have welcomed at the time. But I knew I had to respond, and with something for which he would have respect. I had been put on the spot several times over the years, most often working in television making split decisions.

It was several seconds before I turned to the most stern face I had run into so far in the book business. I looked Mr. E. right in the eye and said, "They may be a lifestyle, but they are a very necessary one. Everyone has to eat." This was a catch phrase my company had implanted in the sales force in our indoctrination. It was also a statement that couldn't be argued with. At least I hoped so. I stopped, hoping my hands weren't shaking, and waited for the verdict.

It was around thirty seconds, during which I seriously considered just running down the steps and out of the store, when who I thought had become an adversary broke out in a grin and put his hand out to shake mine. I had passed the test. I was accepted by the great man, even though I represented something known as non-books. He would never let me forget that, and he even had some good sales on my celebrity books. We became friends and it stayed that way until Mr. E. died at age 89 in 1991.

He loved to have lunch at Musso and Frank Restaurant right down the street from The Pickwick, also on the Boulevard. Of course everyone knew him, and to lunch with Mr. E. here was like lunching with a celebrity, which, of course, he was. Its bar was a regular meeting place for famous and would-be-famous writers. Most couldn't afford to eat there but they couldn't not afford to be seen in this bar, especially those who wrote for television. I watched many a deal made here.

On my way to take him to lunch, about two months after our initial meeting, I'm rounding the corner from Highland Avenue to Hollywood Boulevard when my peripheral vision caught sight of my cook books filling the main window of the store. It was a spectacular display of all the titles that I was told later sold a ton of books. Mr. E. quickly picked up on my beaming over what he had done for me. When I thanked him for the display, he said, "You're welcome, but they're still non-books," with a big smile.

I had heard that Mr. E. attracted all the famous Hollywood types, including William Faulkner, F. Scott Fitzgerald, Aldous Huxley, as well as Charlie Chaplin. They came to the man because he knew just about everything there was to know about books, and he freely shared this with anyone asking for advice. The man regularly wandered through the store looking for someone with a needy look on their face. He loved books and he loved people.

The classic dignitaries, above, were there long before me, but by coincidence, Harry Morgan, who was the second colonel in the TV series, MASH, seemed to be around on many of the occasions when I was. He was apparently an avid reader with an active interest in multiple subjects, and seemed to enjoy getting into discussions with customers, as well as Mr. E. One day when I was talking to the boss, Morgan walked up and we started a lively discussion on the politics of the 1960s.

The Pickwick Hollywood store—closed in 1995—was the symbol of how you bring the written word to a self-absorbed town, Hollywood, that in those days was completely focused on the silver screen and the rising popularity of television. Eventually Mr. E. had to think of the future and sold The Pickwick, with all its branches, to the B. Dalton chain, later to be gobbled up by Barnes & Noble. Would you believe there is a Starbucks and souvenir place where the Pickwick once reigned?

And the last Hollywood Bill Ballinger story involves the Highlander's Horace, again, that I promised earlier. We had come to the Ballingers' house for an afternoon pool party and dinner one weekend. It was after dinner, and we were sitting around talking when the doorbell rang. Since we were the only guests with no others expected, who could it be at this late hour? Opening the door, Horace said hello to Bill's wife and Lucy treated him like a long-lost friend.

She invited him in and it was kinda like old home week for a while until we all got caught up, and Horace revealed the reason for his visit. He was somewhat guarded as he asked us if we needed any sheets or pillowcases. He told us he had a truck idling outside, a semi that had been hijacked earlier tonight and abandoned by the hijackers. We could take what we wanted and he would be on his way. Now this is a scenario that could only happen with a master of the impossible like Horace.

Of course, we declined, but we all had a good laugh over it and this is the last time either Bill or I ever saw Horace.

Although I was really a small fish in a big pond, Southern California was good to me, particularly after my company bought a couple of publishing firms that published "real books," as Louis Epstein would call them. The original Dr. Spock came from one, the other developed Phyllis Whitney, a well-known mystery/suspense writer, only to lose her later to Doubleday. She would eventually become a huge bestseller in the mystery genre of fiction.

But celebrity books were making it big at the time, so we got on the bandwagon with names like Ronald Reagan, Eddie Cantor, Harold Lloyd, Jimmy Durante and Ruth Waterbury, who at the time was writing the Louella Parsons column. I didn't meet Parsons personally but when visiting her home in Beverly Hills with Ruth, I could hear her shouting instructions for the column from her bedroom upstairs. I also set up all the publicity for the book, "Candy Hits by ZaSu Pitts," and still have a copy.

The above titles are now only a vague memory, but there is a special story for each, my favorite being an afternoon spent with Eddie Cantor. I was there to get some background on him to promote his book, and he took me into a narrow room where the walls were lined with pictures of the top stars of his day. He saw me eyeing one autographed by Al Jolson and asked me if I was a fan. In the moment, I was completely dazzled by all the photographed pictures of major celebrities.

I told Mr. Cantor I thought Jolson was the greatest entertainer ever, then realized what I had just said. He looked at me with a smile and said not to worry. He understood, actually knew what I was thinking, I figured, replied that he half agreed with me. He said the other half thought he was a pretty good performer himself and I agreed. I asked him how he got the name "Banjo Eyes," and he immediately rolled his big eyes around for confirmation of the nickname. Nothing else was necessary.

After we had spent over two hours talking about Jolson, I remembered why I was there. We needed to talk about his book, *As I Remember Them*. The autographed copy is still in my ex-wife's possession, as are other of the celebrity books I worked on. I discussed how we would handle the promotion as well as some specific bookstores where it could be purchased in Hollywood and Beverly Hills. Cantor, of course, mentioned Pickwick, also Walter Martindale's Beverly Hills store.

Mr. Cantor listened attentively, asked no questions, and seemed more interested in just talking about his life in show business, almost as much about Jolson. His health was not good; I had witnessed him taking a large regimen of pills earlier. He also looked and acted very lonely, as if I might have been the only person he had had contact with recently outside his household staff. It was hard for me to imagine how a great entertainer such as Eddy Cantor could be lonely, but I also saw this with other celebrities.

He was too big a man to need sympathy so I was very careful not to show any. We concluded our conversation and I thanked him for his generosity, once again telling him what a great entertainer I thought he was. Mr. Cantor thanked me by giving me an autographed picture of Al Jolson; he had already signed a copy of his book. This was after his beloved wife, Ida, had died in 1962, and in October of 1964, Eddie Cantor died of a heart attack.

Harold Lloyd, now, was a different story. He was all business, and I was sorta like the servants. Summoned by phone by Mr. Lloyd to his home to pick up some promotional material for his book—*Harold Lloyds World of Comedy*—I fully expected to be greeted by some secretary, handed the material, and left to go my way. I was met by the man, himself, and invited into a darkened hallway. I was anxious to ask him about some of his silent films, but it was obvious there would be no small talk today.

He asked me to have a seat on a sofa, telling me he would return in a minute. I was determined to see more than just the hallway, being in the home of a famous comedian that ranked up there with Charlie Chaplin and Buster Keaton. I stood up and was on my way down the hall when I brushed against the velvet tapestry that hung from the wall. Dust went everywhere. There was an obvious spot on the drapes where I had brushed past and I knew I must do something to cover my tracks.

My first thought was that I should try to even out the absence of the area where the dust had been disturbed, but I only made the situation worse. I was busily attempting to figure out how to rectify what I had done when I heard Mr. Lloyd address me from behind. He said, "Here is the material, and please stay in touch." Handing it to me with no obvious concern for the dust spot, he turned and walked away again. I left, and that is the last time we talked.

Chapter Seventeen: I Worked With a U.S. President

Last, but certainly not least, there was my tour with Ronald and Nancy Reagan, and I use the term because it was like enlisting in the Navy. You didn't know what to expect when you signed on, the duration was long, and it was good getting out. All kidding aside, this was the publicity campaign that taught me the ropes, and it was kinda fun. He would become President in 1981 and serve to 1989. This was 1965. It was made clear from the beginning by Nancy Reagan that I would be "working" for him.

The name of the book is, *Where's the Rest of Me?*, the title taken from the movie "Kings Row" delivered to Ann Sheridan when Reagan's character discovers he has lost both of his legs. In the book, the title represented the actor's unrest as a Democrat and liberal, and his abrupt change to the Republican Party as a conservative. Although critics considered *Kings Row* Reagan's best movie, the book had mediocre sales, but everyone was anxious to interview Reagan.

From my association with him over the period of a few months, I can confirm that the man was dedicated to his cause. And Nancy Reagan was completely dedicated to "Ronnie," as she would adoringly refer to him when I would call to set up publicity. They were living in Pacific Palisades at the time, a community located on a bluff overlooking the Pacific Coast Highway that paralleled the ocean. The autographed copy of the book, also in my ex-wife's possession, is now worth $2,350.00.

One of Reagan's first appearances was on the "Bob Crane Show" in Hollywood at KNX/CBS radio. I had been bringing Bob guests for a couple of years and he trusted my judgment. You have to understand that at the time Reagan was still considered just a B movie actor, but having had some TV success on "General Electric Theatre." He might have been serious about politics, but politics wasn't yet serious about him, including the media. It wasn't that easy getting him on even the local shows.

He was on Crane's show with a writer for the Red Skelton Show, Sherwood Schwartz. Reagan kind of took over, and he and Crane bantered back and forth for a while on the people they knew in show business, and at one point Bob looked at me to let me know he was getting ready to drill my guy. He did, looking Reagan right in the eye and saying to him, "Welcome to the right side of politics." At first Reagan wasn't sure how to respond but eventually realized the significance. From there it was all uphill.

Bob Crane was a Republican but had a liberal streak when it came to peoples' rights. This came out during the show, and Reagan made it clear that he hadn't firmed up his conservative philosophy yet. But it was the Reagan Doctrine that governed foreign policy in the 1980s in dealing with a communist Soviet Union in the Cold War. Not long after that, Crane jumped to television with his hit show, "Hogan's Heroes." Morning radio in Los Angeles was never the same without the "Bob Crane Show."

It wasn't long until conservatives were beginning to line up to get a piece of Reagan, realizing how his celebrity could bring instant fame to the Party. Walter Knott's group in Orange County—yes, that's the Walter Knott that started Knotts Berry Farm in Buena Park, California—was one such following, and they set up an autographing at a Tustin, California, bookstore. Reagan's daughter, Maureen, called me and said she would join us because I think she sensed her father's inexperience in publicity.

To begin with, Reagan got lost and I had to go rescue him at an off-ramp a few miles South of Tustin. A small crowd had formed when we got there, and after all the introductions were taken care of, Maureen came over to me and whispered, "We've got to get him out of here," meaning her father, "these people are John Birch Society." She had overheard conversations Reagan hadn't. Why hadn't somebody checked this out in New York where the event had been scheduled?

If you don't remember, John Birchers were ultra conservatives, accused of spreading Communist conspiracies propaganda using McCarthyesque tactics. Walter Knott was known to be a sympathizer. Maureen was getting frantic, but I convinced her that yanking the man right now would only make a scene, as well as some enemies. We waited it out but monitored the conversation very carefully. Apparently no real damage was done, since he did go on to the Presidency.

The John Birch Society might be compared with today's Tea Party in their philosophical beliefs. Birchers were also accused of racism and anti-sematic views and were clearly a group representing the radical right. As then House Speaker John Boehner attempted to separate the GOP conservatives from the Tea Party radicals recently, Maureen Reagan sensed then that we should distance her father from the extremist right of that period. In recent years the John Birch Society has not been influential.

Before marrying Nancy Davis, Reagan had been married to Jane Wyman, Maureen being a product of this marriage. I was sitting home one night and got a call from Nancy Reagan, my first, as this was the beginning of the publicity campaign. I had just received a box of fifty copies that day of *Where's the rest of me?* Ms. Reagan had just received her first copy. As most celebrity books of this period did, they had placed several pages of pictures in the book.

She was very businesslike and came right to the point. "I want you to remove all the pictures of Jane Wyman from the book." Caught off guard, I replied, "I beg your pardon." "The picture of Jane Wyman," she repeated, "Take it out of the book." Frankly, I hadn't paid much attention to the centerfold of photos in the book. I quickly got my copy. There she was, and I hurriedly began to try to figure out how to handle this situation.

The silence must have tipped Ms. Reagan off that I was thoroughly confused, so she said, "Just cut out the page with that picture." That made my job somewhat easier, but the books in question were for publicity contacts and I wondered just how they might react to a page missing, especially a photograph. The bigger question was how my employer would make the changes to the books already in print. It was too late to call publicity in New York, and I decided that was their problem.

I knew I had to be as precise as possible to avoid the deletion being detected, a job that took me well into the morning to finish. I left home early the next day and headed to Hollywood for a round of appointments with TV, radio and newspaper folk. These were people I knew and they trusted me, so I was not about to deny what I had done, which could have opened a can of worms. At the end of the day and after eight sessions with contacts I had known for some time, I was just a little bit doubtful of the potential success of this book.

In not one instance did anyone ask me about the expunged page; not even an incident where they took a long look at the spot where Jane Wyman had been expelled, if they even got to the point of opening the book. Don't know if they really didn't notice, or just didn't care, but I am inclined to go with the latter, since in my experience the company's lifestyle books elicited significantly more interest. Not even a follow-up telephone call to inquire about the droll source of Nancy Reagan's concern.

This would be a pre-cursor to the interest in this and all the celebrity books published by my company at the time, and eventually they decided this genre was not their niche. It did, however, give me a firm foundation in book publicity, and how to handle the media. It was quite easy to get someone's attention when you said you have a book about Eddie Cantor, or Harold Lloyd or Jimmy Durante. But the key was then walking in the door with something of substance.

The company had given it the old college try, however, with celebrity books from Ronald Reagan to Eddie Cantor, to Harold Lloyd to Louella Parsons. And the latter would put me in contact with one of the most fascinating people I would meet in Hollywood. Parsons' gossip column was written in later years by a diminutive, lovely lady by the name of Ruth Waterbury, who owned two large dogs, either one of which could have eaten her alive in one bite.

Each time I visited Ms. Waterbury regarding her Parsons' book, I would spend at least a half-hour on the floor playing with the dogs. And during this interlude the second lady of gossip would ply me with stories about the Hollywood celebrities and their antics. Like how a major TV production company had to lock their series star in the studio during filming because they were afraid his gay exploits would get him in trouble. She also shocked naïve me then with the fact that Johnny Mathis was gay.

There was one more instance of Ruth Waterbury's tales out of school, which was centered around her backyard and the steep rise at the end. By the way, none of this was told to me in confidence and was apparently known throughout tinsel town's in-crowd. Douglas Fairbanks lived just up this incline, and when they held their wild parties, guests would get so drunk that some of them would get too close, lose their footing, and roll down the bank, eventually ending up at Ruth's backdoor.

She would simply put them in her car and drive them back to the party. Ruth told me there were many repeaters, and over the years the number of famous people who rolled down that bank would have made a great book in itself. It was never written, as far as I know. Ruth was also the former editor of *Photoplay* and *Silver Screen* magazines and covered the Hollywood film industry for over 50 years, going back as early as the late 1920s. And, she was a five-time president of the Hollywood Women's Press Club.

The other thing I took away from this California experience was a unique ability to drive from Hollywood to my home in Huntington Beach, late at night, with a finger closing one eye so I could focus on the road. It was a talent that stayed with me until that crucial day when I quit drinking. I also employed this technique while imbibing in Des Moines but apparently needlessly, since I only saw one cop the whole time I lived there. Although this worked for me, now I realize what a fool I was for doing it.

Before leaving the subject of Southern California, I have to express my feelings for a place that took me in and welcomed a Southern boy from the country without any questions or reservations. Los Angeles is like that, and the romantic in me says that you can criticize L.A. all you want to, but there is still a mysterious vitality in this huge metropolis that you don't find in New York, Chicago, San Francisco or any other large city. Los Angeles, with all its problems, has a built-in charm that is unequaled.

Most people live there because they love it, and many of them are transplants from all over the United States who decided to give up the East or the Midwest, or the South or the Southwest or Northwest for this La La land. I treasure the time I spent there and to this day cannot really figure out why I left. Twice.

Chapter Eighteen: Into the Snake Pit

But moving ahead I felt I must. However, I always thought that when you did a good job you were rewarded. This publishing company did just the opposite. They sent me to Des Moines, Iowa. OK, there was a promotion to Sales Manager of the book division, but hardly adequate to overcome the fact that I would be living in Des Moines, Iowa. I have family and friends that still live there and I apologize to them in advance about my depiction of their city.

I didn't even like the Midwest, except for Chicago, so you can imagine my hesitation when moving to Des Moines in 1965, with temperatures at below zero. I wondered how people stayed warm in this kind of climate, and it didn't take me long to find out. They drank a lot, and I don't mean hot chocolate. I am talking about the hard stuff, booze, and lots of it. And, I'm not sure it was simply due to the cold. I suspect there was a great deal of boredom involved.

The first morning I reported for work, I didn't know where to park so I had to stop at a gas station across the street from my new employer to call my boss to find out. The parking lot was in the back-forty of the building, which was built in the 1920s, if my memory is correct. It looked like it inside and outside. If they couldn't afford a new building, I wondered what else I had to look forward to. I discovered they had just installed air conditioning.

The guy I worked for, Fred, we'll call him, is another of those best kind of people you run into so rarely in life. He could have made it anywhere but was born and raised in Des Moines and determined to succeed at home. Besides, there was no way you would get him too far from his favorite watering hole, the Firebrand. It quickly became a haven that would allow me to survive this God-forsaken place. At the Firebrand, you found and met new friends to drink with in a city I found basically unfriendly.

I realize I have lost many readers from this city—possibly the whole Midwest—that seems to attract presidents, but if you have gotten this far you might want to hang around because it does get better, and you may find out things about Des Moines you didn't know. But as far as the presidents coming there, I can't deny that these folks were considered the typical American family and most of the time use good common sense. Unfortunately, this was a trait never found in my drinking habits.

The Firebrand could have been the prototype for the bar in the TV series "Cheers." It was *the* gathering place for the Des Moines in-crowd, and Herbert, the owner and bartender in those days, made it just as hospitable as Sam Malone did his place on television. The waitresses catered to the regulars, and if there was someone you didn't know, you would by the second drink. But once again, I am getting ahead, and we need to go back to my first day in the corporate office.

Fred took me over during the morning and introduced me to the company nurse, Wanda, which kind of puzzled me until it was made perfectly clear the next day. There was also a physician that came in part-time to give examinations to new employees, but it was made clear by Fred that Wanda was someone that I would want to stay on the good side of. Then, on the way back to our offices, Fred told me we had a problem. I couldn't imagine what I had done in that short period of time to cause trouble. I hadn't.

It seems that my next door office neighbor had taken the time to compare my office size with his, him being senior to me in the company. This guy had actually counted the number of 12-inch-square tiles in his enclosure, then mine, and determined that I had one more row than he did. It wasn't perfectly clear at that moment but became apparent very soon that corporate life was not for me. Laurence Peter said it best that people will tend to be promoted until they reach their "position of incompetence."

The partitions were about six feet tall, and I couldn't believe it when maintenance moved the wall on a line one foot toward my side. This company had paid to change this partition just to appease a paranoid employee? I told him, "let's change offices," but he would have none of that, preferring to make his point. So began my corporate life. I finally got even, though. When drinking together one night he put a twenty dollar bill in a piano player's tip bowl, mistaking it for a single. I saw what he did but said nothing.

Up until the day he left the company—it was before me—we never discussed his tacky complaint, but I did tell him I had seen his mistaken tip, and I considered us even. He was completely blotto over what I was talking about, and afterward always looked at me in a strange way when we ran into each other. He's the same guy who, when plastered at one of the company's sales conferences, put a child's toy rattler on his forehead with a suction cup, walking around afterward with a red blotch where it had been.

But, back to the rest of my first day. After all the official indoctrinations were over, Fred and I sat down and talked about just what we would do to excite the sales force. The book division had always been a stepchild to the magazine, and would, unfortunately, remain that way long after my exit. This was a problem that demanded attention, so we went to lunch. At the Firebrand. It was about twelve-thirty, and I anticipated probably returning in about an hour. Dreamer.

That was Monday. On Tuesday I learned why I had been introduced to nurse Wanda. She was the holder of the Alka Seltzer, and that was the key to surviving a day after lunch at the Firebrand the previous day. That lunch, by the way, turned into an afternoon of drinking, which turned into an evening of drinking that resulted in the Tuesday hangover. Wanda was reluctant to pass out too many of the fizzies, reminding Fred and me it wasn't good for your heart. That was the least of my problems.

To say the least, I wasn't very welcome by my wife at the motel where the company had placed us until we found a home to buy. We had two rooms; one for my wife and me and one for the three kids. Apparently, I had a key to both, and ended up in my kids' room. When I finally got into bed, I couldn't figure out why I had two wives. Then I realized it was my daughters. They were used to their dad drinking while we lived in California, just not this much. Not a good start.

It was soon after that I had to hit the road and travel with my sales force. I had no idea what to expect, but it was obvious that in this new position I must inspire some kind of work ethic in these guys that would make management proud. The sales force had listened to me when I was in the field, when we got around to being serious about company matters. But, I have to admit that as a rebel, I didn't always agree with company policy, even as sales manager, and would often agree with their complaints.

Now I was no longer one of the gang, I was a leader. How do you all of a sudden separate yourself from those all-night drinking fests with your peers at sales conferences? Since these events were a drinker's paradise for the guys, sort of to let loose while management was bombarding them with new books and strategies to sell, it is amazing what we got accomplished. Being the easy sort I was, this translated into days on the road where martini time still beckoned no later than 5 PM.

Once I was headed out to Atlanta and had a stopover in Chicago's O'Hare; in those days you couldn't fly anywhere directly from Des Moines. I was waiting for my flight and, of course, sitting in the bar having a drink. Right across from me a crowd was gathering and I noticed the center of attraction was Muhammad Ali talking to a group of young boys. All of the kids were black except one who was white, and he was standing back, not participating. Don't forget, this was the mid-1960s.

Ali talked back and forth with and answered questions from the black kids, but you could see he was concerned about the one non-participant. In a few minutes he walked over to the white kid, kneeled down, and shook hands with him. He couldn't have been more than nine or ten, and I have never seen a child light up like that before. The great one also whispered something in his ear, which changed this kid from a wallflower to a member of the group. From then on you couldn't shut him up.

One quick antic of office humor. Our division ordered only one subscription to the *Wall Street Journal* and passed it around using a routing slip. As a practical joke, I started a rumor that someone in management was going to leave the company and was looking for a job. Next, I watched the distribution of the *Wall Street Journal* by the messenger person delivering it and other mail to the offices. It went to other executives before it went to the targeted person.

I was several more names down the line. Very nonchalantly, I removed the paper from the guy's inbox when his secretary was gone and took it to my office. I quickly cut out from the "Help Wanted" section several job offers that would befit the level of expertise found in our office. Watching closely, I returned the paper to the box I had removed it from and waited. The idea was that the next stop for the WSJ would be the vice president.

The day after, nothing had been said, so I repeated my exercise, and each following day for the rest of the week. Now it was Friday, when the proverbial newsprint hit the fan. When I came in on Monday morning I found out there was a meeting going on between top management and the subject was who was planning on leaving the company. Not that they didn't expect it, considering the fact that everyone in this division considered themselves underpaid.

One of the sayings about being employed here was, "It's a nice place to work, if your family can afford to send you." That line spoke volumes about the pay scale.

Unfortunately, the hammer fell on the guy that preceded the V.P. on the routing slip; he was actually behind closed doors with management when I arrived at work. Feeling really bad about the situation, it was up to me, the culprit, to make this right. That meant finding someone new to serve as a sacrificial lamb, but I figured it made no difference, since using multiple victims on the routing slip would certainly give everyone a clue that this was a practical joke. It didn't.

The very next day I proceeded to undo my wrong by hanging the albatross on another guy in another department, which took considerable cunning to accomplish, since I had to schmooze with secretaries I didn't know that well. Being the calculated practical joker I am, I was able to pull it off but without the effect I had hoped for. As indicated earlier, they still didn't have a clue and just transferred the investigation to the new department.

At the outset, I had to drop the hint to my original target that someone might just be playing a joke on us. The term "us" was used to try to include myself in the non-suspects group, but I am not sure if I succeeded. The guy eventually convinced the higher-ups that he had no intention of leaving the company, probably easy, since he was actually from Des Moines. But he always looked at me suspiciously from then on until I finally left the company. Nobody knew about this until now.

Chapter Nineteen: A Sewer Runs Through Des Moines

On a trip to Atlanta, my sales person picked me up at the airport and we went to a motel where we were sharing a room; something that had been arranged by the salesman, which I never quite understood but made me wonder about his intentions. I would soon learn that I had nothing to worry about, as this guy apparently was just trying to impress me with his economy. Once settled in the room, off to the bar, then dinner, then more drinks. Finally back to the room and crashing in bed.

There was a small closet in the room and in the middle of the night I heard this pounding noise coming from inside. When it didn't let up, I went over, opened the door, and found my sales guy on top of a woman who turned out to be a hooker he had ordered. It seems the bellman was a friend of his, and knowing he was on an expense account, guaranteed the tips would be good. It looked like my guy was finishing up, so I decided to use the bathroom before going back to bed.

Right in the middle of my taking a leak, the hooker walked in, said hello, and went over to a bidet in the room and cleaned herself up. I never figured out why there was a bidet in the room, and when I jokingly asked my salesman, he told me that before this he hadn't even known what a bidet was. Of course, I had been offered sloppy seconds and said "no," but was more concerned why he used the closet. I was told that on this first meeting he didn't want to keep me awake. So much for my first road trip.

The Firebrand is one of those unique places where you actually go to see friends and end up consuming a lot of booze in the process. The latter was a necessary evil in my whole scheme of things, but I could only hold so much before the world turned into a fairyland. That's what happened to me at what I called the "transition hour," and from then on my functioning closely resembled talking to Alice in Wonderland. This was the phase just prior to baby talk.

In the course of an evening, we might decide to change bars and leave the Firebrand for some dive, a classification for which Des Moines was noted. One was on the East side of town and had semi-nude girls dancing on the bar. I was there numerous times, actually had drinks, but until this day could not tell you what the place looks like, nor do I remember ever seeing any of the dancing girls. This is called phase 2, when the childish gibberish comes into play.

It was after this phase my one-eye driving learned in California came in so handy. Sometimes I would decide to head home while in this phase, knowing full well that what came next was an alcohol coma. Somehow, most of the time I had the reasoning, although terribly limited, to prevent this. In phase 2, I always drove at speeds that would defy the act of crawling, and I was amazed that I was never pulled over. As a matter of fact, during my three years in Des Moines, and as I indicated earlier, I only saw one cop.

On one occasion I drove home and parked half way up the driveway, leaving the engine running. I must have sat there for some time because the next thing I know, my oldest daughter is turning off the engine and pulling me out of the car. It was in the middle of winter and I had the windows closed tight. Someone told me later it wouldn't have taken long for the carbon dioxide to do great damage or worse, bringing a screeching halt to my drinking days forever.

But there were times that I made it into the driveway, even all the way into the garage. We had one of those partitioned garage doors that rolled up, but had never put an automatic opener on it. I had to unlock it, turn the handle, and throw the door up where it usually stopped at a certain point. The guy who built this house could not be considered a "quality" builder, and this was only one of many problems. Once, in a torrential rain, the downstairs rec room flooded because he hadn't flood-proofed around the house.

Apparently, over time the flange on the garage door that terminated its forward motion had weakened. This one time it didn't stop and rolled right off the back of the roller suspension, falling on the garage floor. How do you explain that to an insurance company? How do you explain that to your wife and kids, whose bedrooms were right over the garage? I didn't. Looking at the pile of door on the floor through buzzed eyes, I pulled the car in as far as possible and went to bed.

I have the three greatest kids in the world. They put up with my drinking and not one of them ever had a problem with booze or drugs, even cigarettes. I would like to think my heavy imbibing had some redemptive effect and that might have been the kids' determination to avoid all my nasty habits. Something I haven't mentioned until now is the fact that, at the height of my drinking, I smoked four packs a day. The whole cigarette. It was automatic.

It only took one sip of a drink to prompt me to light up. Starting from martini time, on most days I had sucked on at least eighty of the killer sticks by the time I packed it in that night. I am so not proud of this since, in addition to the stupidity of my antics, it caused my current state of asthma and COPD, either of which could eventually be fatal. As you know, I ceased both of my most favorite habits at the same time on the same day. Not bragging, just confirmation that it can be done.

To give you an idea of my kids' indulgence of my boozing, the two girls were having a sleep-over party one Friday night, with everyone congregated in our basement family room that had ground-level windows looking out on the front yard. There was one large window right by the front door. Bushes lined the windows in front of the house. My son's bedroom was also downstairs, and the spirited little guy he was, he no doubt was right in the middle of the merriment.

This particular night I made it no farther than the driveway, and then I had to surmount steps up from there to more steps that led into the house. I was able to climb the first set, but in the process of making it to the front door on the second set, I lost my footing, and fell onto the ground with my head protruding through the bushes, looking directly into the family room. At one of my daughters and her friend! I do not remember their expressions but do know that mine was an alcoholic euphoria mixed with regret.

I think I made a Burt Reynold's commitment—from one of his movies—to never do that again, knowing full well that I would be the topic of conversation at my daughters' school the next day. Some of their teachers did have an occasional drink at the Firebrand, so my reputation was at least somewhat known. The Firebrand had a network, sorta like a grapevine, that guaranteed a complete loss of anonymity. Anyway, like Burt, I reneged on my affirmation, but always checked the kids' party schedules in the future.

Usually when you hear the word, commodore, you think of something with class. This was not the case for the Des Moines Commodore Hotel, in an otherwise upscale neighborhood, that had a swinging bar in the basement in an old room that, like the rest of the hotel, was just…old. Not that I would really know, because I have never been there sober. It was another one of those, "I'm tired of the Firebrand, let's go somewhere else," places. I ended up there already half schwacked.

We just proceeded to get drunker at the Commodore, and I think the drinks were slightly cheaper. It was my habit over the years to switch from martinis before dinner—assuming there was ever any dinner—to Scotch/water after, then stick with the Scotch the rest of the evening. I think my problem was that I liked the taste of Scotch, and I still fancy its smell. And there are several ways to drink it: on the rocks, with water, or with soda. I once even knew someone who drank it with 7Up. Ugh!

One night when leaving the Commodore, and trying to find my car in the parking lot to the rear, I wandered off the hotel premises and into a residential yard next door. It was unfenced and as I maneuvered aimlessly, I thought I heard clucking. To this day I do not understand why I thought my family had all of a sudden acquired chickens. All I can figure now is that I must have decided it was my house in my drunken stupor. I actually tried to get in the back door, and, fortunately, didn't wake up the folks that lived there.

Unable to make entry, I returned to the yard to find a place to sleep, since my wife had obviously locked me out. Now that didn't bother me as much as the fact that my backyard had apparently been turned into a farm, fully stocked with cackling birds. You should know that I was wearing a black suit, which, of course, shows any dirt, especially the lighter kind. Particularly noticeable would be chicken droppings that most people, even drunks, wouldn't expect to find on their clothes. So why do I even bring this up?

In searching for a place to lay my head for the evening, I had somehow crawled beneath a chicken coop in this family's backyard. Most likely, I had simply been looking for a roof over my head and concluded that three chickens would suffice. As I said earlier in this book, what the hell are people doing keeping chickens on their property in this upscale Des Moines neighborhood? None of my business, apparently, since it wasn't my yard and I was obviously trespassing.

You cannot imagine what it is like to awaken when the sun is just coming up and realize you are looking up at the butts of three chickens, suddenly recognizing where you are. It was the house right next to the Commodore and in the search for my car in the adjacent parking lot, I had meandered into this yard. Either the family wasn't up yet or out of town. There was another alternative. My reputation had preceded me and this family, including their chickens, wanted nothing to do with an enduring drunk.

I did my best to leave unobtrusively, taking with me on my clothes the droppings, which the poultry family had expelled during my stay. I was lucky; they had miraculously missed my face. Finding my car right where I had left it, and without even brushing off my clothes, I got in and drove home. I parked in the driveway and went into the house, dropping chicken dung along the way. I threw my clothes in a pile and crawled into bed. Thank God, this was Saturday morning.

When I finally got up later, the clothes were gone. So was the rest of the family, taking advantage of the weekend. I quickly tried to figure out how to explain the condition of my clothes to my wife, then wondered how the hell to explain it to the cleaners. But the most important thing at the moment was a cup of coffee. As I nurtured the brew that repeatedly brought me back to life, and what I would eventually refer to as my "brown martini," I pondered just how long I could keep this up.

Coffee was my only connection with survival when I had been out on a night of hard drinking, arriving at the office with a monumental hangover. It was like finding an oasis in the desert after spending days walking aimlessly in the hot sand. I consumed anywhere from ten to twenty cups on a bad hangover day, depending on the severity of my besottedness, placing my devoted assistant in the precarious position of showing up at the coffee urn so regularly she soon had her own reputation.

Chapter Twenty: This Nightmare Can't Last Forever

Hangovers are something that some poor souls are proud of because it is a measure of their ability to handle their booze. This reaction is reserved for the most serious, and I might add, the most addicted to the bottle. In other instances they are a dreaded retribution for a night that particular individual might just want to forget. In either case, they are guaranteed results of serious imbibing for most. That is, unless you have had so many you become immune. This actually happened to me.

I was on a trip with my Detroit salesman, and after work we ended up making just about every bar in the Motor City. We capped the night off—actually it was around 2 AM—by eating the greasiest bowls of chili outside of Texas before calling it an evening. The next morning I was leaving to return to Des Moines, and while getting ready to leave had the feeling I was forgetting something. I turned the room upside down opening every drawer, even looking under the bed, finding nothing I had missed.

It was my proverbial hangover. I didn't have one. I wasn't feeling great, but wasn't experiencing the usual nauseated and headachy condition I had always felt in the past. Must be the chili, I thought, but whatever it was, it was a good feeling, and maybe I had stumbled onto something. After some careful research, I decided it wasn't the chili. The only way to really test my theory was to get drunk again. No problem. Once I returned to Des Moines I would immediately launch an investigation.

What better place to conduct my examination than the Commodore in Des Moines, where the drinks were actually strong for a reasonable price. A couple of guys from corporate and I headed out after finishing up on a Monday, and pretty soon the booze was flowing and we were all well on our way. I was sitting at the bar with one friend on each side of me. The one thing about Des Moines was you never had to look far for a drinking partner. They were readily accessible.

The one on the left was having a conversation with the guy to his left, when I heard the stranger say to my friend, "You're a schmuck." My friend started laughing like he had just heard the funniest joke in the world. Then he turned to me and said, "What's a schmuck?" When I told him, he looked like he wanted to fight, but since he was half the size of the other guy, and a lot drunker, he decided to keep quiet for the rest of the evening.

I, in turn, continued with my test, and consumed several more Scotch and waters to make sure my analysis of the situation would be a valid one tomorrow. In other words, I embarked on a path to inebriation that would provide conclusive results for my experiment to determine if I somehow had developed an immunity to hangovers. I got smashed. However, in this case, even in the apex of inebriation, it was clear to me that I must stay on Commodore property and not the farmyard next door.

I was up bright and early Tuesday morning, but now in the role of a scientist with a goal to revolutionize the drinking lifestyle. And, the same thing that was missing in Detroit, minus the chili, was still missing in Des Moines. A hangover. To be quite honest, it was a bit frightening when you've suffered so many years with this aftershock to a glorious evening of imbibing. I almost hoped it would eventually hit me so I would feel secure in knowing I was suffering as a typical dedicated tippler should. It didn't.

Drinking as much as you want without a hangover…who could ask for more? It goes without saying that to feel this way the actual act of boozing has to be as important to a person as the camaraderie that normally is associated with this routine. To this day, after years of sobriety, I still do not know why I oftentimes drank just to get drunk. Maybe it had something to do with loosening my inhibition, to what, I am not sure. If it had something to do with my exposure to boozing as a young boy, I am not aware of it.

My parents did have parties where the liquor was flowing, and I was offered a sip by several of the merrymakers that at the very least put me in the "happy" playpen. And later, before I actually started hitting the hooch, I can remember getting a glass of soda and sitting down somewhere to pretend I am at a gathering having a drink with friends. Nevertheless, the catalyst must have developed that eventually turned into a serious drinking problem that had to be dealt with.

So then it was back on the road traveling with the sales force, with no threat of the God-awful sequel to hundreds of hangovers I had had over the years. I didn't let it bother me at the time, but a bartender in Omaha once told me it was just plain unnatural not to feel awful after an evening of drinking as much as he witnessed me putting away. I thanked him and moved to another bar my second night in Omaha. This bartender, while a more sympathetic woman, still questioned my theory, but with the motherly approach.

During this period, each time I hired a new sales person—it was always guys in those days, don't remember a female ever replying to one of my ads—I would travel with him for a week in his territory. When I was new, my boss came to travel with me in Memphis, and it was before I had received my company car. We were using my personal automobile, and the very first call on the very first day, I locked my keys in the car. Although this guy was a prince, he jokingly referred to the incident over the years.

The two of us later proceeded to fly to New Orleans, where we would work and play for the rest of the week. We made some good calls and decided to wrap up the week with a liquid tour of Bourbon Street before returning to our respective homes. This was completely effortless, as the bars, lounges and restaurants are side by side for several blocks. Mission accomplished. Since this was before I was rendered hangoverless, on a call the next day I did something else neither of us will ever forget.

While attempting to introduce the boss to a client, I stuttered and stammered, only able to come up with the customer's name eventually in the introduction. It was touch and go for a minute as I tried to regroup and settle both my mind and stomach. We sat down and did our business, the client merciful in giving me a good order, no doubt out of pity for my condition. We left, and while on the way to our rental car, the boss said, "Forgot my name, didn't you?" To which I replied, "Hell no, I forgot my name."

But one of my most trying experiences was with a salesman in Cleveland. I believe W.C Fields said, "Last week, I went to Philadelphia, but it was closed," which also sorta applies to Cleveland. This guy was infinitely horny. Once, while he was at corporate, four of the female staff complained to me he was constantly hitting on them. In Cleveland we shared a room, due to a convention in town and his lack of planning. Naturally, we headed out after work for an evening to absorb as much booze as possible.

Also in his sights was picking up a woman and having a threesome, or ménage a trios, as it is referred to in French. At that point in the evening I was just drunk enough to go along with the idea, and finally my lascivious sales person scored. We headed back to the room with a relatively good-looking gal that was obviously stoned herself. But had I been just a little more sober, a drunk female would have been untouchable. There were no preliminaries; the guy encouraged her to take off her clothes, which she did.

When I looked at her condition, some modicum of decency seemed to return, and when he started to take off his clothes, I decided I couldn't take anymore and left, without even a nod when closing the door. The bar was closed, so I sat in the lobby of the motel for a while, then returned to the room. I could hear the commotion going on several rooms away. There was an argument over what this joker wanted the girl to do, which, even as drunk as she was, she was having none of it.

I told him to wrap it up so we could get some sleep, but he was concentrating on his conquest, which was really going nowhere. I slammed the door and walked out into the motel courtyard, where I encountered a very docile, looked like a large lab dog that was loose and unattended. Now I am a real animal lover, but the urge was irresistible and I felt sure no harm could come to the dog. I coaxed the animal over to the door to the room, opened it, and ushered the dog in and once again slammed the door.

It wasn't long until the young lady staggered out, half dressed, and still very drunk. Apparently Fido had shown up beside the bed with a very loud slurping sound as the girl was still resisting and scared the shit out of the both of them. Returning to the room, I went to bed. But first I had to find the dog's owners, which I did. My sales person did not mention the incident the balance of the trip. Eventually I had to fire him anyway for hitting on clients.

Our sales force was made up of twenty-two guys at one time but was whittled down to only seventeen, adding more geography to each of their territories. It was hard to get good men with what we were willing to pay, but I managed to recruit a great bunch that did good jobs with annual revenues always increasing. I didn't coddle these guys, but I did make it a point to listen to their problems and regularly took these back to my bosses in Des Moines.

Of course, in a sense, the home office was a big part of the problem. Corporate concentrated on selling advertising in its two magazines and adding more radio and television stations to its broadcasting division. Even the printing division got more attention than books, but none of them had more fun. Like I said before, we played hard, but we also worked very hard and sometime the higher-ups didn't understand this. Even so, I soon discovered this perpetual alcoholic playground was going to kill me.

Chapter Twenty-One: Drinking in a So-So Stock Market

As I indicated earlier, during my management years the sales conferences were legend, and I always dreaded the annual one in Des Moines. It always involved top executives of the company who were treated like royalty by my bosses. The hardest task I had during the meetings was the seating arrangements for a formal dinner. Just letting the people come in and pick random seats was out of the question. Someone might be sitting next to the wrong someone, whatever that meant.

So it was my job to come up with a seating chart, designating where each individual would park him or herself. That meant these folks had to wander around the banquet room looking for their names, alternately bellowing across the room to tell a friend that they had found their seat. Management's purpose was to mix people up so they could meet someone new, but all these folks were interested in was the free drinks and food.

Each sales conference was regularly graced at least once during the meetings by the corporate President and Chairman of the Board, who would come to one of the hospitality suites held for company VIPs. I had to make sure Heineken beer was available for him, but my sales force wasn't allowed to touch the expensive brand. They were limited to Budweiser and Schlitz. Occasionally I would see one of the guys sneak a Heineken, but the maverick in me said nothing.

After a few Heinekens, the President would turn philosopher, wanting to talk directly to my troops, which they relished, as a way they hoped to get to top management. By this time the men were successfully bombed and were making little sense to each other, much less what they might say to the company's top executive. But this was how the hierarchy feigned a comradery that was basically fabricated for the situation. Little did the men know that in every case they would simply be the listeners, not participants.

In our first "corporate get-together," my boss and I decided to sit in and see just what kind of encouraging advice the old pro would pass out to a bunch of guys who were primarily interested in getting on to the next drink and a serious game of cards or craps. A group of about six guys gathered around the Prez and his Heineken and waited for those gems of inspiration. It would be an experience for both Fred and me that would bring to a grinding halt our participation in the future.

He started by telling us how he started with the company in sales and progressed up the ladder, eventually ending up in the home office in Des Moines, and then was lucky, and apparently highly qualified enough, to make it up to President and Chairman of the Board. With the rapt attention of his audience, he proceeded to persuade these guys that all they had to do to exceed was to work hard and walk the company line. Not once did he mention that he had very tight connections.

It was getting deeper by the minute with his admirers' attention spans looking more and more challenged, but as I noticed the urges to defect for another drink, I quickly countered with a look that said, "don't you dare." Our VIP, already into at least his third Heineken, was getting his second wind and continued with what he had been able to do for the company and just how important it was coming up through the ranks. Once again, left unsaid was how much easier this is starting near the top.

What he failed to say throughout his long dissertation was the fact that he had married the daughter of the founder of the company. Talented maybe, but this sort of made him a slam dunk, right? This was never openly discussed with the sales force but some of the men did know. Other family members would move into this position over the years and eventually there were none, but the firm would finally realize that there was some pretty spectacular talent available within and eventually use it.

The Prez finally felt like he had made his point, from the confident look on his face, when he asked if he could have just one more Heineken, with which I quickly accommodated him.

Then, with a very serious look on his face, he turned to the salesmen I had labored so carefully to hire and said, "I hope you are all happy in your jobs, but if you aren't, you can just quit and we can hire someone for a lot less money." Those aren't the exact words, but you get the idea. Fortunately, this didn't do a lot of damage.

At that point, all six guys looked at me and I quickly released them from their required presence in front of our dear leader. One by one they sauntered off as the CEO looked around the room in hopes of cornering six new recruits for indoctrination. If he didn't find a ready audience he would address several guys at a time and wave them over until he had covered the entire sales force. This happened at every sales conference held in Des Moines, until the man retired.

I talk about Des Moines like it is a third-world country, as my daughter, still living there, once told me. I don't mean for it to sound *that* bad, and I realize much of the blame for my attitude resides at my feet. I still have family and friends who live there and the old town I knew in the days I am writing about has really blossomed, as I found out while attending two granddaughters' weddings. But I still could not bring myself to go back to the Firebrand for fear I would be disillusioned.

Gallons of booze later, I left this job, which had been good to me but didn't have the future I was looking for. Still not sure what that was, but at the onset of a new group of management, the emphasis turned to a more serious side of selling, and I later heard the days of wine and roses was soon a memory. Regardless of the sometime intemperate imbibing, we sold a lot of books and always beat the prior year's results. Had I been as serious about my job as I was about drinking, who knows what could have happened.?

What is so tragic about the next move that I made is the fact that I would have to remain in Des Moines. When you bitch and moan as much as I did about the place where you lived, wouldn't you think I would have the sense to leave? Well, I didn't, so there is no one to blame but myself. It just reconfirms the lack of direction in my life and with the gypsy blood still boiling, I was to remain here, if for only a short while. Somehow, I don't think I'll ever shake the gypsy mantle.

But then, for some dumb reason I decided I wanted to become a stock broker, studied for the position, and passed my state exams. I joined a small firm in Des Moines and was introduced to a whole new set of people, one of which shared my habits. Harold liked to drink and was very good at it. We became instant friends. This is yet another example of how I attracted those who fancy a drink or two. Or three or four or five or six, or just ad infinitum. But I do think the feeling was mutual.

His specialty was commodities. He was an expert and made a generous living off that and stocks. He was already a frequenter of the Firebrand, where I had met him but only in a casual way. We immediately staked our claim to a table at the favored watering hole and quickly attracted a dedicated entourage of fellow drinkers. It was even better than my old drinking days with the publishing company. The New York Stock Exchange closed at 4PM, EST, which meant in Des Moines 3 PM-plus became martini time.

And we were destined to continue Herbert's luck of attracting regular drinking customers who also summoned their friends. This is because people like to belong, and, as in the TV show "Cheers," our crowd knew they belonged at the Firebrand. Except I was no longer on an expense account and didn't make anywhere near the money my friend did. Regardless, I never did cut the volume intake of booze. But he did get me more into beer, which was cheaper.

One night my friend told me the story of an Iowa farmer who took a long commodities' position in soybeans, not from him but another broker in our firm. The customer was new at trading and didn't completely understand the delivery catch. The broker had dropped the ball, and the farmer had to take shipment of a carload of beans at maturity. This isn't the way the commodities market is supposed to work. The broker should have sold the beans before delivery, at a profit when the price went up.

Something was eventually worked out between the customer and the brokerage firm, but it confirmed my belief that I should stay away from commodities trading. I could just see myself working a position in, say, corn, and missing a delivery date due to a long lunch at the Firebrand. All of these things, combined, sealed my doom as a stock broker. Since I had no idea why I had gotten into this line of work, except the fact that I wanted to get away from the publishing company, what the hell, nothing was lost.

Although corn is an Iowa staple, and I do really like corn on the cob, I couldn't see my family consuming the number of bushels of corn in a commodities position. If we were still in the South, I would have sold it to moonshiners to make "white lightning" and made a lot of friends and money. Geez, I could have even gone into business for myself with my own still. But it was inevitable that I would give up selling stocks, but not until Harold and I spent innumerable nights at the Firebrand together with friends.

He was not a nomadic drinker. He liked to stay in one place…the Firebrand. The ambiance in those days was questionable and the place wasn't really that big. It was like a smaller bar than "*Cheers*." That's the reason we established our position at a table, and the waitresses seemed to know when we would arrive and had our site for indulging available. And indulge we did. Harold was older than I was and I couldn't figure out his stamina, until one night he told me just how he did it.

He exercised, running at least two miles every morning, regardless of how much he had to drink the night before, and he invited me to join him the next morning. I did, and for several months I felt great and was able to keep up with my friend in our drinking bouts. It was easy in the spring, even most of the summer and fall, but come winter, even though I was working up a sweat, I could never keep warm. Not sure whether it was the weather or just the Des Moines thing in general. I finally gave it up.

Chapter Twenty-Two: The Epitome of the Peter Principle

There were several evenings that, during several drinks or beers, or both, Harold and I would brainstorm with our group of imbibers to come up with ideas for what might be the next fad, like the pet rock was then. In my case, this was a classic example of being bored out of your mind, grasping for anything. One idea was to sell those plastic sheets with bubbles in them that were used for packing. We would market them in five by five foot lengths, calling them "Pops."

The point was to place the plastic piece on the ground and stomp on each bubble, which produced a popping sound. We even brought a sample to the Firebrand one night, placed it on the floor and proceeded to demonstrate our new invention. Pop, pop, pop, until Herbert allowed as how we were annoying his other customers and asked us to stop. We talked about it for several weeks but our genius of creation never went into production. It's easy to forget while on a steady intake of booze.

There was yet another flashing brainstorm that also went nowhere. This newest endeavor into commerce was based on something that had happened on a live TV show: a guy had dashed through the scene in back of the host…naked. The media picked it up and designated him a "Streaker." So why not start a "Streaker's Club," charge for membership, with the requirement to stay in good standing that the member had to streak somewhere in public once a year.

You have to remember that these were still the days of Barnum & Bailey, where "a sucker was born every minute." And this was a conglomeration of guys that for some reason or other elected to go to the Firebrand every night after work instead of going home to their families. I remember once in Memphis, the wife of one of my drinking buddies decided to drive to the bar where we were drinking and sent his daughter in to roust us.

But to round off an interesting night of non-stop drinking, it was always special when two particular traveling salesmen came to Des Moines, whose first stop was always the Firebrand.

Over the years, even before my time, they had become two of Herbert's regulars and aside from their most unusual professions, always had stories to tell. They were one of a kind, literally, representing trades that at least in those days were unique. And I would wager a bet that you would never guess what they represented.

One of these guys was a soot salesman, who came to Des Moines because there was a tire company there and soot, at least in those days, was required to make tires. He explained the process meticulously one night, but most of us were too far gone to understand, or care. What was interesting was that my wife then worked for one of the executives at the tire company, but I never mentioned this because, as I said before, none of us was really listening to the salesman.

The other guy was a stem salesman. Because the natural stem on a maraschino cherry would disintegrate in the liquid in which they were packed, it was necessary to manufacture a plastic stem and insert it into the cherry. They would last until the cherries were used and would easily pop off the fruit when consumed by the drinker. On one evening, we were all indoctrinated in the precise method of placing that plastic stem on the cherry, delivered by our friend, as if anyone gave a damn.

Herbert listened in on one of these conversations once and finally walked away convinced, based on how intent our attention was to these innocuous subjects, that we had all had enough to drink. He didn't cut us off then, but he usually kept a close watch on the intake of his regular drinkers and at least attempted to coax them into quitting or at least slowing down. I am sure that if he felt the person was incapacitated, he would cut them off and take their car keys. Sometimes it didn't work.

One of those nights, I was the culprit, when a friend and I cornered two gals from the publishing company where I had worked. We knew both of them but were also aware that both of them were married. C'est' la Vie, so were we. The evening progressed and all four of us were getting successively drunker. The two ladies had had enough to drink that they agreed to go to a motel with us but insisted it be on the northeast side of town, away from where any of us lived.

My car was parked out back of the Firebrand where I had also seen my friend park her car earlier. There were front and back doors, and I headed out the front when my friend reminded me our cars were in the back. That should have been a major clue, but I was determined to take advantage of my conquest. We both turned back into the bar and headed through to the back door. The gal said to follow her, as if she had been there before, so I got into my car and did what I was told.

The fact that I had mastered one-eye driving in California came in handy once again as I tried to navigate carefully behind this young lady who was at least as drunk as I was. Things were happening in front of me that were, to say the least, confusing, but I continued on. My quest for amour was running at full speed and I was determined not to lose out on this stroke of good luck. My lady friend worked in a different division of the company than I did, so I wasn't concerned about potential gossip.

We meandered through the streets of Des Moines in neighborhoods that I had never seen, but if they weren't close to the Firebrand, I wouldn't have. I just hoped I wasn't close to my house, because at that point I would not have recognized it. In this case, Herbert had not anticipated my level of inebriation. We continued, or at least I thought it was "we," until I noticed there was no car in front of me. The street was completely clear of any automobiles. And then I saw it.

Looming directly in front of me in the middle of the roadway was a house being moved. Yes, I mean the kind they build on a piece of land, right in the midst of one of the main thoroughfares of a metropolitan area. Good God, it could only happen in Des Moines. And, it was heading right toward me, not fast, but just enough that had I kept going, I could have ended up on the front porch. It was my determination that this liaison was over and I carefully made my way home, which took at least two hours.

My once willing friend never showed up at the Firebrand again; in checking I found out she did make it home that night and perhaps her husband put the clamp on her drinking for a while. I don't even remember her name and she probably forgot mine soon after this incident. You might say it was a couple of drunks passing in the night. Nothing really romantic, just two horny people trying to connect. I told the Firebrand crew about almost running into the house during our next liaison, but no one believed me.

The stock market wasn't for me and I finally concluded, neither was Des Moines. I told the Firebrand crowd I would be leaving town soon, which was received with plans for a bon voyage blowout. One roaring night a bunch of friends from the publishing company and the brokerage firm started a drink fest parade that included all the bars I had frequented during my stay. Once completed, all my friends wished me well and I went home…I thought. I woke up in a super market parking lot the next morning.

I had recently lined up a job in the junk mail business based in Chicago. It had been giving the traditional retail business competition and looked like a great career. For the time being the family would stay in Des Moines while I found a place for us to live in the Windy City. In Chi I ended up in a dilapidated old apartment building on the Near-North side, on the second floor with no elevator. It occurred to me that these stairs would definitely be hard to negotiate after a night of drinking.

The Peter Principle says, "in a hierarchy every employee tends to rise to his level of incompetence," meaning, that many companies have a habit of promoting workers until they reach a position in which they are completely inept. The concept was spawned by Dr. Laurence J. Peter and Raymond Hull in a book of the same name that poked fun at the decisions by corporations to move workers from positions in which they held at least some competency to one in which they were totally unequipped.

I had worked for a few, but my next experience was, well, just that, a real experience. If not for the fact that I met the woman there that I would happily spend the rest of my life with, I would say the whole adventure was a bust. It was my entry into the junk mail business, where I would stay for 35 years for the simple fact it offered me such a great living. My wife-to-be, Barbara, was working at this personal data center in Chicago when I joined the company in 1969, which made the struggle somewhat easier.

I quickly learned that when in town there were no martini lunches, not even a bloody Mary, so my midday meals were usually at my desk, or just skipped altogether. This abstinence was not prevalent, however, when we hit the road and the guy I worked for, very possibly the one Dr. Peter patterned his principle after, turned into another person. It wasn't a radical shift, just enough that you knew the next few days were going to be interesting, at the very least.

With Fred at the publishing firm, you knew where you stood. This guy was so ineffectual he constantly kept you off balance, both when we were in our office and traveling together. No matter, at least there was my martini, and pretty soon I was able to tune him and the rest of the mostly boring clients out. The boss, who had friends at the corporate level, was a stickler for all his salesmen wearing hats, but not once did he give me any direction in marketing our products.

Chapter Twenty-Three: An Almost Lunch with the Mob

On the other hand, this data company introduced me to a guy in Minneapolis who was an absolute pleasure to work with. Together we were able to poke fun at my boss without him really knowing what was going on. The client was Irish, and, once again, one of the good people of the world. He was in a position of giving me a tremendous amount of business, and did, but never let me know he was in control. He, along with Barbara, were the only two people that made working at this company bearable.

One night this guy and I got obliterated, making the bars in Minneapolis and St. Paul. I should note that he handled his booze extremely well and became more careful driving the more he drank. This particular evening he finally dropped me off at my hotel, the Northstar Inn. Downstairs, there were shops and parking, so you had to negotiate the elevator for the reception area, where, of course, the bar was. Just one more drink. I staggered into the bar, then almost fell off a stool.

I remember the bartender asking me if I was staying in the hotel, and when I produced my key to pay for my drink he looked relieved I didn't have to drive anywhere. When I finished, and before heading out, I cautiously inquired from my host where the elevators were. "Out the door and around the corner to your left," was his answer. I was on my way to the "house." But first I had to negotiate getting out of the bar, which was somewhat cramped and full of people.

Heading for the elevator, a door opened, a man exited, and I walked in, the door closing behind me. It locked. Not the elevator. A stairwell, and a quick realization that I was locked inside. What the hell, I thought, I need the exercise to work off the booze, so up I went, unfortunately not counting floors. What difference did it make, all the doors were probably locked, which was confirmed on the next level. What the hell again, I was so drunk I could have slept on a lighted fire pit.

Just stretch out in the stairwell and someone was bound to find me eventually, which they did, and promptly called security. After confirming I was a guest in the hotel, and being helped to my feet by the security guard, I proceeded to my room. Oh, by the way, the security guy in a very critical tone of voice also told me all I had to do to open the door was to use my room key. I looked back at him half sobered up and said, "BFD." He definitely did not understand drunks.

My Minneapolis friend also had another talent he had developed about as good as his ability to hold his liquor. He could talk as much like a gay person as the real thing. Now, please don't think either of us was homophobic, because we are exactly the opposite. I believe vehemently in gay and lesbian rights, and am positive the friend was not prejudiced in any way. When you're drunk, shit happens. My gut tells me that with the steady flow of stories this guy had to tell, he was just a frustrated actor.

We went to a gay bar in St. Paul and he pulled off an act that could have won him an academy award. He wasn't bad looking, with broad shoulders and masculine features that appealed to another patron at the bar. He told me to just say nothing and act as if I was too drunk to be picked up, which was a snap in my condition. After a while, though, I felt just a little self-conscious, since I was the only one at the bar not being hit on. Not that I wanted to be, well, you know how one can get insecure over the craziest of things.

My client talked to his buddy for about a half hour, then without warning told the guy he was not gay, just putting him on. I nearly dropped my drink because, even drunk, I knew this would piss the guy off and start a fight. It did. Collectively, we fought our way out of the bar onto the street where, fortunately, there were two cops, one of which my friend knew. It wasn't until later that I learned this was the way the scenario went when he was plastered and fessing up was a part of the plan.

So was life in the fast liquor lane. One night Barb and I were out drinking late into the morning and finally went back to my apartment to freshen up for work. We headed out late and I was really pushing it to get to the office on time. We came up behind a bus, which made a sudden stop, prompting me to slam on the brakes. In those days I wore a hairpiece, and when the top of my head slammed in to the visor, the "mouse"—an endearing term I used for it—had to go somewhere.

It ended up over the front of my face with the adhesive used to hold it in place on the top of my head now sealed to my nose and cheeks. At first I thought I had gone blind! We had a laugh and still got to work on time, although terribly hung over. We have memories of several of the nights where we would end up early in the morning at an IHOP eating steak and eggs. Chicago never slept. Barbara has always accused me of first introducing her to the martini and then coffee to sober up from our regular soirées.

In another "mouse" incident, I was in the old Kansas City airport somewhere in the 1960s waiting on a connecting flight to Des Moines. I was very hungover, the airport wasn't air conditioned, and I was wearing a mouse. It was the kind with a plastic base with a clearance of about three-eighths inch from my head. Sweat had formed, and a fly decided to take cover there. It crawled up under the hairpiece and began to prance around on my head, causing unbearable itching.

Without thinking, I began to pound on the top of my head to try and scare the fly out. There were two little old ladies sitting right across from me and immediately their hands flew up to their mouths when they saw what I did. My prior effort not working, I did it again. The ladies quickly got up and headed for an airline counter across the terminal where they approached a representative and then they pointed at me. Had to do it again, so the guy saw me pounding on my head. Didn't seem to faze him.

He talked to my two friends who didn't seem impressed with what he said, and then they cautiously moved to another side of the terminal as far away from me as they could get. The fly was still driving me nuts and I was still hammering my head for relief, when the culprit finally walked out and flew off. All was quiet as I watched the two old dames who still did not take their eyes off me. Then they called my flight and on my way to the gate, I could see the relief on those faces that they weren't on my plane.

The manager of the Chicago office of the personal data center threw an annual Christmas party for all the employees at his home in Deerfield. He was Norwegian and always brought out the Akvavit, a Scandinavian liquor that, when consumed straight, as it was supposed to be, could quickly deliver one to Utopia. I decided at the first of these events Barb and I attended together to show everyone that I could hold my booze. However, it was not to be.

Now I'm a big boy and responsible for my drinking habits, but the host knew I was driving, yet he continued to shovel the Akvavit down both Barb and me. I matched her, and most of the other guests at the party, two for one. Finally, we started home, after deciding Barb was the soberest. It was raining like hell, and when she became concerned over her ability to negotiate the roadway, she pulled over to the side of the road. Barb has always been the level-headed one in our relationship when it comes to drinking.

Inevitably, the Deerfield police spotted our car stopped along the roadway and the cop gently and courteously knocked on the driver side window. The inside of the car must have smelled like the distillery that produces Akvavit, but we weren't driving, so he didn't give us a ticket. But they had to get us off the side of the road where someone—maybe another drunk— might rear-end us. I must add right now that the Deerfield, Illinois, police are the greatest I have ever run into.

The officer moved me to the backseat—I was passed out and oblivious to what was going on at the time—Barb moved to the passenger side, and he drove us to the police station. His partner followed, neither of them, I'm sure, ready for what they were about to encounter. When the cop awakened me, I made it difficult for him to get me into the station house, but eventually quieted down on Barb's advice. She allowed as how they weren't ticketing us, rather, just taking us in until it was safe for one of us to drive.

Inside it was quite different. I grabbed the younger of the two cops and demanded that he get me a package of cigarettes. He did. I didn't even pay for them or thank him. Then came the lectures, during which I made it abundantly and belligerently clear that we really shouldn't be here, it was the boss's fault. After that, sobriety tests for both Barb and me. When they had the results, it was decided that Barb could drive after an hour or two, and several cups of coffee.

When he looked at me, the verdict was that I would not be able to drive a car for at least two weeks. Eventually they released us, me in Barb's custody, and said they did not want to see us again. Little did they know. As I indicated earlier, these two cops were the epitome of professionalism and must have had a great sense of humor. There is no doubt in my mind that I must have entertained them for one of them to take the time to go get me cigarettes and not ask me to repay him.

Well, you may think my story ends here, but it doesn't. The very next year there was another party, same place, with another more than adequate supply of Akvavit. You would think I might have learned something from the prior year—and perhaps the host might have known better—but, naturally, I didn't. But then, neither did the party-giver. Fortunately, Barb did, and backed way off the shots of the Norwegian's dynamite. Now the party was over again and we left.

It was another dark and stormy night just like the year before, and, even though Barb had refrained from drinking too much this time, the weather forced her to pull over to the side of the road. And you guessed it; the cops came along again to find out what was going on. What you might not have guessed, it was the same two policemen from the prior year, and worse yet, they recognized us. Especially me, slumped and passed out on the passenger side.

Since Barb presented herself as reasonably sober, and because, once again, they appreciated the fact that she had the common sense to pull over and park when she knew she was impaired, they decided to test Barb right there in the rain. I remember waking from my stupor temporarily and wondering what the hell she was doing walking around in the rain. Soon after I blacked out again. She passed, and both cops told us they *really* didn't want to see us again after this time. They didn't.

This company did provide me the opportunity of almost having lunch with the mobster, Sam Giancana, once. I was out with one of my suppliers of paper products during the Christmas holidays at a restaurant on Harlem Avenue in Chicago. The waitress serving us quietly pointed to another booth in the back covered with a curtain. Mostly as a warning, she said Sam Giancana was in there with one of his lieutenants having lunch. In other words, we shouldn't do anything to disturb him.

As the lunch progressed, I got drunker and drunker—I was celebrating the fact I had told the company I was leaving for a much better job with more pay in California—and it became harder and harder to stay in the slippery leather seat. We never had lunch, and the next thing I remember is Barbara helping me off the floor from under the table. Not only had I spent much of the afternoon under there, I had missed Giancana's exit from the restaurant, passing right by our table.

Chapter Twenty-Four: California Calling...Again

I would have done just about anything to get away from "this" company, and something did come along that was an opportunity not to be believed. One of the junk mail business' oldest premiere catalogs beckoned, and I said to Barb, let's go to California! Chicago is a great city, but between the weather and an employer that I progressively hated to come to each day, it was time to leave. We had recently been married and Barb had not really traveled too far from her birthplace of Chicago.

The new company was located in one of those classy beach communities named Playa del Rey, a suburb of Los Angeles, in hopping Southern California. The corporate building was a magnificent structure called the "Taj Mahal" by those of us who worked there. The guy who founded the company had started on his kitchen table in Connecticut, eventually deciding to move west. My office was spectacular, and I decided I had arrived, settling in as the new Marketing Manager.

I soon discovered that this was the real mail order business, the term I used in those days until I finally figured out it was, in fact, junk mail. At the least, ninety-eight percent of the catalogs I would put in the mail every year ended up in the trash can. Most people cannot wrap their minds around that figure in relation to how the industry made any money. And, if it weren't for loyal customers ordering on a regular basis, and the selling of your name and personal data, there would have been no profits.

The first day in the building, my boss took me out to lunch and proceeded to order a martini, looking at me as if I had better follow his lead. I did, and just when I thought we would order lunch, he ordered the second martini. Following suit, it became apparent to me that no work would get done that afternoon. When he ordered his third, I just looked at him and knew I was in trouble. By then I was ready to blow off the afternoon but quickly learned that he was better at this than I was.

We returned to the office, and my lunch partner immediately called a meeting, including me, and appeared in complete control of himself. My participation was pathetic at best, and it was then a decision was made. If I planned to make this job work, no more lunches with the boss. Fortunately, our apartment was close enough that I could at least feign having lunch there with my wife, even if she didn't show up. It wasn't long before I got the name, "Noon-e-Dunning" for going home for a nooner.

It wasn't that I didn't want to drink my lunch, I did. It was just that this was the first week on the new job and my common sense told me I couldn't keep up with my superior. In the past it had always been me that had led the way for the drinking conglomeration. Had I finally met my match? If so, it was best to abstain during the lunch hour. I welcomed the "Nooner" rep, but it didn't always happen that way. And I quickly made up for missing imbibing at lunch with several drinks in the evening after work.

We lived in a resort-type apartment complex, which was in the Palms district of Los Angeles, and because of its close proximity to Marina del Rey, a real upscale area, it was a very desirable place to live. Completely gated, it had a television connection in each room so that residents could see to whom they were opening their door. The pool area was first-rate and you felt like you were in your favorite holiday spot. Our apartment had a balcony on the pool, providing access to a perpetual bikini-land.

We settled in and my wife went to work for a Beverly Hills dentist, whose patients were many of the stars in the entertainment industry. People like Cher, Jackie Cooper, Nina Foch, Bill Dana, Suzanne Pleshette and Playboy's Hugh Hefner. Now some of you might not recognize all of these names, but keep in mind this was some thirty-five to forty years ago. They were big-time in those days. Barb had become accustomed to leaving Chicago by now and we both decided LA was the place for us.

It wasn't long before I found out about the regular spring and fall conferences held by the Direct Marketing Association called the DMA, which was the industry's lobbying group. These meetings were held in swinging places like Miami, New York, Las Vegas and Los Angeles. This was apparently kept completely quiet by the Chicago personal data company, since the only one I ever attended was in Chicago, where I lived and worked.

My first convention with the catalog company would be in San Francisco, held at the Fairmont, one of the city's most prestigious hotels with a history dating back to the 1906 earthquake. It was nearly completed before the quake hit, and the structure survived, but fire destroyed the inside, delaying the opening until 1907. It was in great shape when we arrived in what I believe was March of 1971. I had been to San Fran and knew where to go but would spend this trip almost one-hundred percent in the hotel.

It was the custom for companies with something to sell to open hospitality suites, a room set aside for each evening where convention attendees could come, have a drink and munch on hors d'oeuvres. I had taken great care to prepare a list of people to invite with the help of one of the brokers of lists, with whom I dealt. I also made sure the food was special, so those who came would talk about the great spread put out by our company. Based on my background I should have known most would come just to drink.

Well, the crowds were overwhelming and did partake somewhat of my inventory of food, but especially the booze. It was the second day of a three-and-one-half day meeting. More liquor had to be ordered and the party continued on its merry way, with it clear to me now that the junk mail business loved to drink. Although I had to maintain at least an outward show of sobriety, it was obvious that I had found where I was supposed to be. This hospitality suite literally put the company on the map.

My boss thought I was a genius at planning this sort of thing and dealing with clients, so I was considered somewhat of a hero by the company staff. I still believe it was at least partly curiosity, since the company had never been highly visible and the industry in general just wanted to see who we were. Whatever the reason, I was showered with telephone calls the week after returning to Los Angeles, with compliments of what a great bash we had thrown

This also opened the door for me to meet all the important people in the business and acquire the reputation of knowing just about everybody you needed to know. It helped over my thirty-five years in allowing me to make the deals I wanted to and in general, get things done. But, as well as I knew many of these people, I was never able to figure out their lax attitude toward the names and personal data it was their responsibility to secure, having almost an apathy toward the whole issue.

Everyone knows that California is the land of earthquakes, with the San Andreas Fault crisscrossing Los Angeles and continuing up the coast. We had only been in L.A. for a short time when during one of my out-of-town trips I get a call from my wife, Barbara, with obvious tension in her voice. She began to tell me about the earthquake they had just had and how she was in the shower when it started. In all the time I had lived in Los Angeles before, I had not experienced a major earthquake.

This Chicago girl was scared to death and proceeded to run out of the shower, still soaking wet with a towel wrapped around her, and head for the outside door to the apartment hallway. She had heard that the safest place was a doorway, and this looked like the strongest one. As she looked down the hall, other residents were leaving their apartments, apparently not the least bit concerned, meaning they were either natives or had lived there a while.

As things quieted down, our phone rang and the caller, a woman, said, "hello honey, are you OK?" Obviously a wrong number, Barb answered, "yes, but who are you?" The woman thought she was talking to her own daughter. As they talked more, it seemed clear that the lady was a very caring Jewish mother, as she immediately began to console my wife. They talked a little longer until Barb graciously thanked her and suggested that she might want to call her daughter now.

This was the Sylmar earthquake in the San Fernando Valley in 1971 that registered 6.6 on the Richter Scale, lasting sixty seconds, causing sixty-five fatalities. The quake was a mere thirty miles from the apartment building where we lived. In my own way I enjoyed them, liked to roll with the motion of the quake, just like sitting on a barstool. But I was never subjected to anything as scary as my wife was. We lived in a house in Ventura on our second stay in Southern California, where all the windows were out of kilter due to quakes.

L.A. was a city of a multitude of possibilities when it came to entertainment. Friday night after work was our "time to swing" as we thought of it, and with Marina del Rey only ten minutes away, a slightly inebriated drive home was not too dangerous. Besides, there was always the old one-eye trick, which I employed on a regular basis. One of our favorite places in those days was called the Second Story, where there was always dancing.

Now I am not a good dancer, tolerable at best…when sober. But after three or four drinks I turned into Fred Astaire, at least in my own mind, and in my tipsy state I was sure that I had mastered every dance step known to man and could execute them with flawless perfection. Barb, who *was* a good dancer, was very understanding and allowed me to ricochet around the dance floor doing my thing. Fortunately, she didn't let me make a complete fool of myself.

Chapter Twenty-Five: Where Do We Go From Here?

Earlier, I mentioned how junk mail catalogs made money, in spite of the fact that ninety-eight out of the one-hundred people receiving a catalog throws it in the garbage. I soon learned where their real revenue came from, and that was the reason why the catalog company had hired me: to sell their mailing list of customers' names numbering at the time more than six million. Junk mail companies could actually lose money selling their products but make it up in list sales. And still have a generous profit.

So, I hit the pavements of New York and Chicago, where most of the list sales people were to sell my company's names. Like in that San Francisco hospitality suite, there seemed to be nobody I didn't know, or, if I didn't, I could make quick friends with on the spot. I soon learned which ones drank the most and specialized in that profile. It also helped that I bought over twenty-five million names a year from the same people I was asking to sell my names. Convenient and shrewd.

My list business boomed, as did my reputation around the company for bringing in some severely needed revenue. But the company would later go out of business. A department store chain in Los Angeles (eventually taken over by a larger chain) had acquired the firm from its owner who had started the catalog in 1951 out of his garage in Bridgeport, Connecticut. The stylish building housing the company was elegantly furnished, from a modish reception area right down to the men's restroom.

Whether it was for real, or an intended part of the décor of the men's room, over the urinal was a picture of an attractive woman with her mouth open in the configuration of a circular pose that was downright suggestive. I asked several people in management if this meant what my dirty mind thought it did, but no one would give me a straight answer. My boss, whose mind was as dirty as mine, said the founder's wife had hung the picture there as a joke. Having met her, I knew she would do it.

During one of the junk mail conventions that was held in Los Angeles, I suggested we hold an open house and invite a bunch of people over for drinks and hors d'oeuvres, along with a tour of the facility. We asked people coming to the meeting to sign up if they were interested. As in San Francisco, we had a stampede, and it was then decided to charter buses to transport the crowd from the convention center. It took three, and we staggered them to insure that we could handle the onslaught.

Department managers were available to conduct the tours to their respective areas, of which many took advantage, but quickly hurried back to the main lobby where the booze and food was located. Once again, I was forced to feign sobriety because I was the one most of these visitors knew and would strike up a conversation with around the bar; I never ventured too far away. As I welcomed the visitors I had the feeling of contentment that goes with accomplishment, one that would fade away in the distant future.

As the evening wore on my discipline faltered, and I proceeded to take advantage of the good Scotch we had purchased for the party, something I personally couldn't afford. At some point, the crowd had dwindled to just a few, so I increased my Scotch consumption. I looked around me and all of the company members but the president were beginning to stagger. The company had had years of success, but apparently this celebration represented the epitome of accomplishment.

Just after the last bus left, returning the remaining passengers to the meeting place, one of the company vice presidents congratulated me on the outcome of the open house. It was beginning to look like a guaranteed future, but even then it didn't feel like the right fit. I was well on my way, but the post of V.P. was definitely further down the trail. Someone else spoke to me then, and I turned to talk to them and during the conversation noticed a horrified look on their face, but looking past me, not at me.

I turned around, and the smashed V.P. I had been talking to had a fire extinguisher in his hand and was advancing across the reception lobby, spewing whatever these things put out all over the walls. It almost looked like he was attempting a design of sorts but not completing his brainchild. Occasionally he would stand back to admire his work, then proceed with the job of redecorating the inside of the building. Apparently this guy couldn't hold his booze, but no one had had an inkling.

The President walked up beside me as our V.P. decided to take his talent down the hallway toward the executive offices. I only hoped that he would spare mine, but he seemed more intent on doing the glass partition behind which the secretaries sat. The Prez kind of smiled at the antics taking place, and I wondered if he would have been so tolerant if it had been me. Fortunately, this was a weekend, and management was able to get a cleaning crew in before we opened on Monday.

When I visited New York I always stayed at the NY Hilton, which was just off Times Square right in the middle of things with easy access to good restaurants and jumping bars. Actually the bar at the Hilton was one of my favorites; one main reason was that you never had to wait for service, with someone always there to take your drink order. It was an open area where hotel traffic was constantly passing, a great place for girl watching. Although I did venture out, the NY Hilton was my home base for booze.

Another reason I liked visiting New York so much was to see a high school friend that I had hired while working at the publishing company. He had been promoted to the New York territory and was always good for a drunken night on the town. On this particular occasion we did many of the bars in Greenwich Village, working our way between each with spurts of rain, eventually ending up at a Nathan's famous hot dog place. I knew I was drunk but didn't think that deserved the weird stares I was getting.

When we sat down to eat my friend told me it was the hairpiece I was wearing. He said when it got wet it smelled like a dead rat, even though it was made out of real hair. Actually, he wore one too, and this was one of his hand-me-downs I had received from him some time ago. I was too drunk to care, and he was too drunk to attempt an explanation, so I just sort of stupidly stared back at my critics who by this time had all gathered on the other side of the room.

The two of us raised hell on yet another earlier occasion during an evening of unbroken imbibing when he was working in the Washington, D.C. territory. We met this gal in a bar and thought she was up for a party, spending a small fortune on food and booze to get her back to the hotel. Finally, she said she was ready to go, but had to stop by her apartment first so, with directions, we took her there and waited out front for her to return. And we waited and we waited.

Well, she never came out, and it just shows you in what part of our anatomy our brains resided during this whole escapade. I was really pissed, so I decided to go and knock on her door but first had to get in the security-locked front door. I hit several buzzer buttons until some lonesome soul let me in and once inside, realized I didn't know her apartment number. Returning to the buzzer bank for a number, I let the door close and lock on me again. At that point I said "screw it" and we went back to the hotel.

At this same time, my list business was setting new records in the company for revenue and I got cockier and cockier by the day. Then I decided if I could do such a great job selling just this one list, why shouldn't I start my own business selling the lists of companies who either didn't want, or couldn't afford in-house representation. I talked to some close associates and eventually came up with the backing to launch what is known today as a list management firm.

I was one of the innovators in this business, with only one other person involved at the time. By the time I left the business the field would be overcrowded, and this specialized area would be absorbed into the regular list selling firms. Since this stepchild of the sale of products and services is so lucrative, most firms hardly ever talked about the fact that when you bought something your name and personal data was on the street for sale in less than thirty days. And it would stay there forever.

So I exchanged the supposed security of a large corporation—the company I left would go out of business in the coming months—for a venture that had all the elements of success, except that it was on the wrong coast. New York was the hub then, and probably always will be, for the junk mail business, especially those selling mailing lists. I was able to attract some major clients, most of them on the West Coast, but it just wasn't enough to pay the bills in the long run.

In the meantime, my new company would garner some decent recognition from the industry and support from those with whom I had worked in the past. Of course, there wasn't that edge that I had experienced when buying lists from those to whom I was also selling, but a name was a name. At least in those days, selling names was cutthroat, with brokers of mailing lists known as "whores." Nothing was sacred, including your personal information, which eventually went worldwide.

In the office I kept a supply of booze in the cabinet in the room that housed the copy machine and water cooler. I could never stand sealed bottles of booze, so I set a goal for the next week of opening one bottle a day and making sure the distiller had done his job. This exemplification should solidly establish me as a versatile drinker, to say the least. There were more than six different flavors of alcohol in that cabinet, all of which I savored like a wine connoisseur, but with the only expertise that I just loved to drink.

After a couple weeks my supply of hooch dwindled rapidly, and I began to wonder if it was all me, or whether outsiders were getting into my stash. I wasn't worried about my office assistant who didn't drink, but there was a cleaning crew that came in every night. So I decided to have the building super put a lock on the door, to which I would have the only key. After this was completed, I waited to learn the outcome of who was drinking all my booze.

It was I, and once confirmed, my assistant told me, "I could have told you if you had just asked me.

Chapter Twenty-Six: Adding Marijuana to the Equation

My assistant, whose name was, let's call her Trixie, had been pirated away from Penthouse magazine, and I could never understand why she would leave the glamour of Bob Guccione's magazine until I realized that she just didn't like working. I found this out during one of my out-of-town trips when I tried to call in to the office repeatedly and got no answer. She explained it off with bathroom breaks, going out to get stamps—we had a Pitney Bowes machine—and various other excuses.

And then the mail person asked me about the office being locked up several times when he couldn't deliver parcels. I confronted her, a good-looking blonde who could have easily been a model, and she acted as if that was just the way she did business. I allowed as how that didn't work for me because clients were now also complaining they couldn't reach anyone when I was traveling. Trixie was very nice to look at but just couldn't combine her good looks with applying herself.

On the next day my prima donna asked if she could take a few days off and said she had asked a friend to work in her place. I never saw Trixie again. And I would never know what she really meant by periodically coming into my office before going home after work, sitting down on the edge of the couch and asking me, "Is there anything else I can do for you today?" In many cases I had already had a drink and am still surprised that I didn't take her up on her offer, just say yes to whatever it meant.

Her replacement was a ball of fire, smart enough to handle any situation, and took over the management of the office the first day as if she planned to stay. She did after we talked, and she broke it to me tactfully that I wouldn't see my lethargic blonde again. But this gal became the dream assistant any business person could ever ask for. Lisa was Black, not quite five feet tall, slim from the neck down with no butt, and sported a shaved head. She wore huge round earrings that dangled precariously, almost to her shoulders.

Everyone loved her.

One of my clients asked her to move in with him. Soon after, I received a call from his boss, complaining about the mixed relationship that he did not approve of. Obviously it smacked of racism, and I told him I would not interfere in the personal life of my employee, but decided I should go over his head to the president of the company, who was a good friend. He agreed with me, and must have said something to this guy, because I never heard from him again; he always snubbed me at industry get-togethers.

One morning I walked into the office late, hung over, after a night of dedicated drinking with an old friend who had come to town. There was a black guy standing at Lisa's desk and they were deep in conversation. I said hello to her and asked about messages, then said hello to her friend. He looked at me with disinterest and completely ignored my greeting. Lisa looked at him and said, "Hey man, he's a 'Brother."

The guy whipped around and shoved his hand out for a shake, and from then on whenever he was in the office, treated me like one of his best friends.

But Lisa had one flaw, and it became obvious one morning when I arrived at the office and she wasn't there. It was only a few minutes until the phone rang, and it was Lisa. She was very subdued and said she had a confession to make that apparently wasn't in her resume. "I am horrified of driving in the rain," she admitted, "You can fire me, but there is no way I could ever drive in a rainstorm." I told her not to worry and that if things were critical, I would pick her up, since L.A. had a limited amount of rainfall.

In later years I came across a Penthouse with a nude spread of my first assistant, Trixie. I reminisced over the days in my office when I would regularly pull out the bottle of Scotch for a late afternoon drink, sometimes before she had left for the day. After a few drinks, when I had worked myself into a state of looped lasciviousness, I would watch her move around her office in tight jeans and T-shirt. There were two things that booze always prompted in me: one was to light up a cigarette; the second was to grow horns.

One of my largest clients was a local company whose head was a good guy with some weird quirks, but the sociable kind that enjoyed lunch with his suppliers. There was a special Swedish restaurant in Beverly Hills that was one of his favorites, and we went there one Friday when neither of us had much to do the rest of the day but eat and drink. The conversation somehow got around to smoking pot, and after two martinis, I told him I had only tried weed once when I was in high school.

I was a kid of seventeen then and was out one evening at a Jackson, Tennessee, roadhouse with two other friends, shooting pictures of couples that really didn't want them because they were both married…to someone else. For years these negatives remained in my files until I finally threw them away. It was then I realized I probably had pictures of some of Jackson's most prominent citizens. On a break, the three of us went to the parking lot and lit up cigarettes. Mine was a Lucky. Theirs were joints.

One of the guys asked me if I wanted a drag on his "cigarette," saying it was special, and with a couple of drinks already in me, of course I said yes. He explained I should take a long, deep drag, holding the smoke inside as long as possible, which I did. Well, bells started ringing and I ascended to this unbelievable high where I was convinced I could fly, which I tried to do in the parking lot. The other guy grabbed me before I ran out in the road attempting takeoff.

I later found that beginners shouldn't mix booze and marijuana.

Back in Beverly Hills, my client and I were finishing our lunch and instead of another drink he suggested we go back to the office for something…different. This would be his very exclusive kind of pot he imported from Mexico that I think he called "wiki wiki." It was supposed to be of the highest quality, and if that meant "strong as hell," I agree completely. Sitting in his office puffing away, I decided I had finally arrived by being taken into this man's personal confidence.

It was interesting that he kept the marijuana in a safe and the building was built like a fort.

I was flying again, and my client asked me if I would be OK to drive home. I said yes, descending the stairs from his second floor location. It felt like I was gliding over the steps but not really hitting them. On the first floor, when opening the front door into the sun, my eyes felt squeezed by the rays, and I rubbed them to try and focus after this jolt. I carefully maneuvered my way to the car and noticed my heart was beating faster and my mouth was very dry, but I was in the most relaxed state I had ever been in my life.

I couldn't sit there in the parking lot forever, so I started the car and slowly eased out into the street, hoping that the gendarmes wouldn't stop me. I can say it now because I no longer drink, but in my twenty years of hard boozing, I was never stopped by the cops when I was driving. Let me make this perfectly clear, the fact that I got away with this for so many years is nothing to brag about. It would have been a disgrace, a tragedy, if I had hit someone while inebriated and hurt or killed them.

But that day there was a certain amount of befuddlement in my head, which was validated when I reached the corner to turn onto the street where our apartment was located. Putting my right signal on, I pulled up behind a car that I thought was also turning. After several minutes I wondered why the car in front of me wasn't moving and gently honked my horn. I expected the driver to move, but there was still no action, so I honked again more aggressively. Still nothing.

But before I could honk again, a guy standing on the sidewalk walked over to the passenger side window, which was open, and asked me what I was doing. I explained that I wanted to turn right, but the car in front of me had failed to move after my already honking twice. The man looked at me and said, "Are you kidding me?" I responded with, "Hell no, I just want to get around the corner and go home." That's when the guy replied, "You're sitting behind a parked car," and walked off laughing.

But it didn't end there. Our apartment building was of the resort type with open hallways to the outside with steps at one end of the hall and elevators at the other. Since the steps were right off the parking area, I always took them, as I did that day. However, I failed to stop at the second floor where we lived, ascending to the third floor and still kept going. The last door, which I later thought shouldn't really be unlocked, led right out on to the roof of the building, where I proceeded to walk right to the edge.

There was no railing, but even in my drugged state I knew I shouldn't walk any further. With the pool staring right up at me, I came to the conclusion that something was wrong and de-addled myself enough to turn around and head for the door and eventually found our apartment. I went right to bed but learned from my wife that in the early evening she had heard a loud thud coming from the bedroom. When she checked she found I had fallen out of bed.

So much for smoking the funny stuff. I stuck to what I knew…booze.

Chapter Twenty-Seven: Annual Trade Shows…Another Great
Reason to Drink

The main thing about the junk mail business I remember
is that a lot of people liked to drink. A lot. Some time, a real lot.
The annual trade show exhibitions occurred twice a year, one in
March, one in November, and they were sponsored by the
industry's trade group, the Direct Marketing Association, the
DMA. They put together a pretty spectacular educational show
two times a year, when many of those attending just wanted to
hit the bar and drink. I was one of those.

I would set up a number of lunches and dinners with
clients, most of who drank. Bingo! My guaranteed martini alibi,
at least twice a day. Some of these "business" sessions ended up
lasting all afternoon, even into the night. One in particular was
being held at Caesar's Palace in Las Vegas. Yes, the DMA did
go all out to provide a conducive atmosphere for its members in
which to "learn." I always wondered why the ads for these
conventions didn't promote booze as the main feature of the
show.

At Caesars, I remember some kind of boat constructed
around the bar area, no doubt for the spectacle. To add to the
boat's drama there was water all around the display. Just deep
enough for someone to get wet, which one of my clients did,
when they went too close and fell in. Being the gracious peddler
I was, I quickly stepped into the water and picked up my friend
who was lying face down. Wet shoes, socks, feet and pants;
didn't even slow down drinking the rest of the evening.

Still in Vegas, but at another hotel, the MGM Grand, and
yet another trade show, but not the DMA this time. This was one
of the major companies I worked with, holding their own
meeting for their agents. They reserved my room, and after
checking in and going there to unload my baggage, I gulped at
the luxurious layout, since I had failed to check the rate on
registering. There was a huge bedroom with a sofa and several

chairs. The bath was almost as large, with a spacious Jacuzzi right in the middle.

Talk about the country boy come to town, but I was terrified at what it might cost. However, this was Sin City, and I had to do a little business and drink a lot so I decided to get started. As I took the elevator down from the sixteenth floor, I wondered how things would work out, as I knew only a minimum of people, and their drinking habits were more conservative than the junk mail gang. Or, at least I thought. On the way down I met a guy from their research department who would convince me I was wrong.

My new-found-friend, we'll call him Stan, said he had just talked to someone in the convention advanced setup group that had been here a few days. They said they had found a bar where the booze was reasonable and the company was great. Within ten minutes we were in a cab on our way. I do not remember the name of the place, but on the inside, it reminded me of a neighborhood bar where the community gathered and everyone knew each other. It was, and at first didn't look too friendly to outsiders.

Well, that changed, and eventually I learned that both Stan and the advanced group guy were family men, and the "company" described didn't mean single, available women, but rather…families. That was fine with me, because I wasn't looking for either and just came there for the cheap drinks. Even though they cost much less than those at the MGM, they still were strong enough. Stan and I were finally invited to join a group of three couples at their table, and soon we were deep in conversation.

I was sitting next to one of the wives who was very attractive and she was way ahead of me on the drinking, so I decided to try and catch up. After three very bold, double scotch on the rocks, I was ready for bear. I don't know what that really meant, but I can get real frisky when I've had enough to drink. I was there, but wasn't ready for what happened next. "I wonder how you would look nude," she said. "I beg your pardon," was all I could come up with, but thought, "Jack, you haven't lost your touch."

To her I must have looked like a high school kid on the way to his first score, I was so flabbergasted. I spied her husband over her shoulder who was talking to someone else. The lady continued, "Ben and I belong to a nudist colony close to Las Vegas and we wondered if you might like to join us this weekend if you're still going to be here." Actually relieved, I answered, "Thanks but I'm leaving tomorrow." I was actually staying through the weekend but I could only see trouble ahead, staring at nudes.

Meanwhile back at the hotel the next day one of my clients asked me if I was planning to go to the nudist camp this weekend. Apparently, Stan had told everyone about my encounter with a nudist, and ten to twenty guys were planning to visit that bar this evening. I did some entertaining and actually got in bed early. It's a good thing, because first thing the next morning there was a fire alarm and everyone was advised to evacuate the building.

The elevators were not working, making it necessary to walk down sixteen flights of stairs, a feat that was guaranteed to clean the booze out of your system. Now walking down from the sixteenth floor you run into a lot of people getting onto the stairs at each level, and many of them were couples. I am not an expert, but I have a hunch that many of them had not known each other until the night before. Fortunately, I did not see any of the management from my client company in the descent.

And then there was New Orleans, a Southern Las Vegas. I had traveled The Big Easy for several years for the publishing company before my latest marriage so I was well acquainted with the best places to drink, many of which were considered tourist traps, but I didn't care. They were either known for good entertainment or excellent service, both of which were important to me. And in those days these bars even charged reasonable prices for the drinks.

There was Chris Owens' Bar, the Famous Door, Pete Fountain's and Al Hirt's clubs, the latter two of which are no longer there. These were strung from one end of Bourbon Street to the other. Then there was Pat Obrien's, where everyone drank Hurricanes and sang along with the music of Mercedes at the piano. You were allowed to take the Hurricane glass with you, and over the years I accumulated several with one still on our bookshelf.

But the most acclaimed place in New Orleans was and still is, Preservation Hall, which was located on a side street off Bourbon where they played authentic New Orleans jazz. You either stood or sat on the floor during my time there, and they did not sell drinks. Can you believe how I ever found, much less frequented, a place like this? I did it for the music, as did everyone else there, which was not like anything else you will find anywhere. It is still there and worth a visit, but not like the original.

When you listened to these guys play, most of which were black in my day, booze was the last thing on your mind. I remember thinking after huge rounds of applause between each number that the audience, many of which were Southerners, cared not a bit that the people they were clapping for were mostly black. This was in the 1960s. Now if people were willing to put their bias on hold while they were giving such a big hand for what was such colossal talent coming from black musicians...well...?

When I had had a particularly hard night of drinking in New Orleans and needed to rise and shine for work the next day, I would head over to Felix's Oyster bar and take down two or three dozen oysters. They had a chili sauce there mixed with horseradish and something else I couldn't determine served with the oysters. It was out of this world, and this, combined with their specially selected oysters, brought in customers from all over the world. This served to partially sober me up, along with a pot of coffee.

During my publishing company days I had to work to justify my presence there, and one of my largest accounts was here, a distributor that sold a lot of my books. The first time I walked in, I was met by the manager's wife, who showed me around and said that she had one rule that I must follow. When I asked what that was, she said, "Just don't fuck any of my girls," referring to those who worked there. I got the message. Actually, considering the prospects, she didn't need to worry.

And then I was passed off to her husband, the general manager of the agency, who welcomed me into his office, offering me a chair. There was a long silence while he sized me up, then abruptly he slammed a 38 revolver on his desk and said, "You've got 15 minutes, start talking." I was not the kind who prepared a canned spiel for my clients; rather, I just went with the flow along with the general direction of the conversation. Somehow my next move escaped me for a few moments.

I don't know what he expected, but I replied, "Man, I've seen much worse from Tennessee moon shiners with sawed off shotguns," referring earlier to the time when I was working on a story for the *Jackson Sun*. There was another lengthy pause while I was getting a steely stare, and then he broke out laughing and came around and shook my hand. This man could make or break me in New Orleans with his control of several retail markets and super market chains.

Now he and I had just become friends. During subsequent visits, and from my home office in Des Moines, there was talk that this magazine distribution agency, as well as others throughout the U.S, had connections to the mob. Now I do not know why the Mafia would be interested in companies that simply distributed magazines and books to supermarkets and book stores, but the rumors were very strong. I didn't really care as long as they sold my books.

The rumors were reinforced by suspicions of the magazine and book representatives like me that what we were saying in the room where the traveling representatives worked was being secretly recorded. Supposedly, when you turned the light on in the room, a recorder started. One morning I walked in and found the lights off, everyone sitting around the table wearing miner's caps with carbide lanterns to illuminate their work. Management wasn't amused, but I do think the guys made their point.

Once again, I have wandered off in a foray of my drinking habits, but it is hard to resist when so many bizarre things happened either as a result of, or leading up to, my just simply having a drink. But suddenly I realized I was becoming bored again and apparently needed to move on. I really didn't know to what, just something else. I was good at the list business but just on the wrong coast. But I didn't really want to move to New York or Chicago.

Chapter Twenty-Eight: Why Not Just Get in the Business of Drinking

All things must come to an end, as evidenced by earlier chapters where I decided to turn a page and move on. My backers eventually pulled the rug on the list management company, refusing to provide further investment money just at the point it looked like we were making at least some progress. I wasn't really sorry, because it was easier to pursue my drinking habits when I wasn't the sole person running the business. Can you believe that excuse?

A company back East in Maryland asked me to merge my talents with theirs, but they were in the philanthropy part of junk mail, where I had always been involved on the commercial side. They were totally dealing with charities and wanted me to attract what I had been trained for to their company. They were what was called a one-stop shop where you could do everything from develop the concept to putting your offer in the mail. They were actually buying my contacts.

But my contacts weren't buying this operation, primarily because of the management types that insisted on tagging along with me on presentations. After visiting several companies, my connections told me that the people I brought with me knew a lot about fund-raising but very little, if anything, about commercial junk mail. The word got around in the industry and eventually it became impossible to open doors.

And then one day I was sitting in my office thinking of our future. My wife was at the time and still is, so patient with my big ideas and new ventures and I was about to have another. Betty Crocker had come out with a series of food recipe cards recently and I suddenly thought out loud, "Why not do drink recipe cards?" I looked around and no one was in view, and I couldn't wait to get home that evening to talk to Barb. After a full explanation she was on board the Jackie wacky express again.

With what experience I had picked up, I enlisted an artist acquaintance for some advice, since the primary hurdle would be superior graphics. This association would eventually sour but we briefly stuck it out with him and his art studio. We hired a bartender to create the recipes for existing drinks as well as invent new ones. My favorite was the Volcano, which consisted of 151 proof rum, vodka, crème de banana, brandy, Galliano and a small amount of orange juice, plus a whole banana.

The volatility of the Volcano closely mirrored my drinking habits.

But first, my departure from the one-stop-shop was sorta amicable, but strained. I told the President, who was a great guy and friend up to this point, what I was planning to do, but I would be leaving the company. He didn't let me finish with the fact that we would be giving all our business, minus the graphics, to him when he jumped in with the statement that my idea was the company's because I had it while working there. My response was, if this were the case, there would be only one company in the U.S.

He didn't agree, of course, but said he wouldn't do anything legally to stop me. Later I found out from our company's attorney that he had absolutely no grounds for action. So we were merrily on our way after securing limited backing from someone that got forty-nine percent of the company and agreed to help us run it. This guy was a heavy drinker just like me and even had a refrigerator by his bed for beer. We had some great momentum, and the drinking public showed no signs of slowing down.

It was Barb's and my job to bar hop with our female bartender, Laurie, to sample drinks and decide how to modify some and devise new ones. Barb drove, Laurie ordered the drinks and I did the sampling. On an expense account. I was in hog heaven. There wasn't one night that I made it to the car without assistance. Other mixologists loved us, and pretty soon we got to know some of them; they threw out the welcome mat when we came in the door. After all, we were spending a lot of money.

The drink recipe card library was named the *Nasty Jack Epicurean Prescription for Spirits,* not really after me, but just something Barb came up with off the top of her head. We launched an advertising campaign through two major metro area magazines: *Washingtonian* and *Los Angeles Magazine.* The response was respectable for print media and with the income we were able to develop four sets of drinks. Eventually, printing, graphics and drink development expenses far exceeded income.

The partner dipped into his bank account as far as he could afford to and then the well went dry. In the interim, we had approached some large junk mail companies that were willing to invest but wanted control of the company to do so. I was borderline but our associate wasn't willing. We even went to Seagram and met with their marketing people in New York but they, as well as everyone else we talked to, wanted to take over. It was soon after that the whole operation would suffer its demise.

But while we were riding high and still testing drinks, there was one that was originally created by Laurie that was almost my nemesis. It was the Blue Hawaii, and it was created exclusively for our drink card library. In it was vodka, rum, Cuarenta y Tres, blue Curacao, cream of coconut and half & half. It is the most delicious drink I have ever consumed, and one evening I just kept making and drinking them. No hangover, but there is no upset stomach worse than one from a sweet drink.

If any of you wants a copy of either the Volcano or the Blue Hawaii just email me at the address in the book.

It's bad enough that I chose drinking as a recreational distraction and spent years trying to turn it into a profession, placing several potential careers like television and publishing on the backburner. Bells should have been ringing and flags going up all over the place as warnings of impending disaster. If that did happen it completely escaped me, or maybe I just didn't want to face the facts. Whatever the case, it continued into an accelerated phase where the drink was the thing. The only thing.

It quickly became a matter of cost reflected in the quantity of booze I was consuming. Now I was a confirmed devotee to Scotch, and as I said earlier, I still love the smell and, I think, taste. But killing a fifth a day became prohibitively expensive and something had to be done. So then I discovered Rhine wine, with a very dry taste that I found I could get used to. Maybe even learn to like it. Well, I did, and little did I know it would eventually be my swan song.

I tried the Rhine wine in a regular bottle size. The first night I realized this would fall far short of my needs. I went out for another, then later, one more. In my Scotch-soaked brain I couldn't reason that the same quantity of Rhine wine does not equal the same in Scotch. So I began to look for an answer to my dilemma, since the single bottles of wine were fast becoming as expensive as the Scotch. And then I went to my favorite liquor store in a Maryland suburb and discovered that Rhine wine came in the half gallon.

Laurie the bartender had introduced us to the manager of the liquor store, who was a nice guy, and gave us a break on the cost of the booze. Okay, now how do you explain the purchase of a case of four half-gallon bottles of Rhine wine? My wife, Barb, came up with the idea that one of the drink recipe card library sets had a selection of party punches and we could tell him it was for that. Pure genius, so we took our dolly to the store and loaded up two cases and brought them home.

Needless to say on future trips, particularly around the fourth or fifth, there was some doubt in the manager's mind just where all this booze was going. The only explanation I had was one I really didn't want to admit to this guy, so I went to another liquor store. And then another. And then another. When it became necessary to go all the way to Virginia to find a liquor store I hadn't been to numerous times, I knew I had to do something but didn't know just what.

Chapter Twenty-Nine: Everything Comes to a Screeching Halt

Several years ago someone told me about the auto dealer philosophy where you sell someone a car, provide lousy service, and the next time they're ready to buy they go to another dealer. They keep doing this over the years and by the time they get back to the one with the lousy service, the buyer has forgotten about it. Well, I used this approach on buying the large quantities of my Rhine wine with the hope that they would forget me. Apparently liquor dealers have a better memory than car dealers.

When one I hadn't been to in some time welcomed me back, I knew the jig was up. But at this point it didn't matter anymore. It's like a druggie who needs a fix, and nothing will stop him from getting it. I was beginning to feel ashamed, and it was a feeling I didn't like. With money running out and facing the fact we would not finish the Nasty Jack drink cards, the inadequacy of it all overwhelmed me. I wish I had done a measurement of just how many glasses of wine it took to forget each evening.

Well, I didn't. And it just came roaring back the next morning and even with no hangover, there are still cobwebs that cloud the issues, and you eventually solve nothing. And that makes it necessary to rush back to the same routine, hoping maybe that it might work this time, but it doesn't. What we have here is an excellent example of inebriated perpetual motion in a cycle that, rather than remain the same, accelerates into a collapse that is both physical and mental.

At the height of all this, my wife, Barb, my partner, and I were entertaining the Maryland regional Manager and his wife of one of the largest convenience store chains in the country. We had a test going on using brochures in his stores at the checkout counter to order the drink cards. The library was in its demise, and this guy was attempting to help us any way he could. I was really in a dazed, intoxicated state thinking about our situation and right in the middle of the dinner I stood up and shouted "FUCK!"

Well, being the nice folks they were, including his wife, they overlooked my faux pas and even invited us to a party over the weekend. When I began to explain, the guy just waved it off as a raucous part of the evening, even said his wife got a kick out of it. Although I had made a complete ass out of myself in front of my wife, she continued to understand my stress, while at the same time she was experiencing the same tension. But as usual she wondered out loud if I shouldn't cut back on my booze intake.

My Rhine inventory was dwindling again and normally I would be planning on a run for more during the coming week. It didn't seem right, the whole thing, I mean. When my head was clear enough—I had nothing to drink the night before—I began to consider what my day consisted of. Very little work on the drink card library, since we hadn't been able to do any additional advertising, and I realized I had been upping my drinking time to an earlier hour and amount with each day.

I looked out the floor to ceiling glass wall of our high rise and noticed a cloudy film on the glass. Rubbing on it left an opening where you could actually see the sunshine that we hadn't really seen for a while, and then I heard Barb behind me. "That's from smoke," she said, but not outwardly implicating me as the smoker. I stood there staring through this clear hole in the smoke-infested glass, seeing trees that were now green in the park out our window. Then I moved over to the gray blur from my cigarettes.

"Did I do that?" I said.

"Guess so, unless it was on there when we moved in," still giving me the benefit of the doubt.

I turned around and looked at Barb, realizing how much second-hand smoke she must have inhaled with my four-pack-a-day habit. She had also been subjected to a similar situation as a child. Geez, I thought, not only am I killing myself...I'm also killing my wife. And then I took the analysis a little further. During the non-drinking portion of the day I didn't smoke one cigarette. The minute I picked up a drink, I lit a cigarette and while continuing to drink, continued to smoke.

Voila! It didn't take a rocket scientist to figure out that if I didn't drink, neither would I smoke. It also meant that if I quit drinking I could also quit smoking. So there lies the rub, and I began to think about how I would slow it down, maybe drinking every other day. That didn't work the first time Friday ended up on my off day. On Friday we always went out for dinner and drinks. There must be a better way. It is amazing the time I put in trying to set up a schedule to drink instead of just stopping.

Okay, how about pushing back the time I started drinking an hour a day until it got closer and closer to bedtime? Well, I handled that by pushing bedtime back as long as it was necessary to consume all the Rhine wine I wanted. Of course, there is always the approach of cutting down on how much I drank by reducing the number of glasses consumed. That was easily overcome by changing the size of a glass to a larger one. Asinine, you say, and yes, I would have to agree with you.

That's when it dawned on me, just buy less of the half gallon bottles and quit when I run out. Unfortunately, there was a deli in the building where we lived that sold booze, and when I ran out would simply go there and buy more. The idea of drinking had become such an obsession in my life that I had a natural ingenuity to overcome any hurdle that stood in the way. It was like a runaway train that could not be stopped, with an engineer that had decided to kill himself and everyone on board.

I explored the possibility of joining Alcoholics Anonymous, which is a great organization, but I am just not a joiner. In later years there was a very close friend who was a member and I remember how he would fall off the wagon and would call me smashed, and I would try to talk him off the sauce; he loved scotch as much as I did. Once, when he had left his home and checked into a hotel for some non-stop drinking, I went to bring him to our house. I told him to stay away from my party supply of Scotch.

He didn't. Barb and I heard noise in the middle of the night coming from the kitchen, and when I went to check what it was I found my friend on his knees in front of a counter, carefully turning my Scotch over and drinking right out of the bottle. He had the DTs, couldn't stand up, and was barely able to hold the bottle. I moved to the other side of the center counter and looked him right in the eyes. I said, "(his name), do you have any idea how pathetic you look?"

There were tears in his eyes, because as one of his closest friends he knew just how much I was hurting with him, obviously not as much, but I had gone through similar circumstances. I don't think I ever went through real DTs, at least not as bad as this. But on many mornings after awakening, when I went for coffee it was necessary for Barb to pour it for me and I had to hold the cup with both hands, I was shaking so bad. My friend eventually went home and later died from an overdose of Scotch. A tragic loss!

Now back to our Maryland high rise and the view out the nicotine-stained windows. I decided that whatever happened, it wasn't going to be bad enough to justify me drinking all the Rhine wine in Maryland. In the meantime, my mother had come to visit us, and she and I got so drunk the night before she was supposed to fly back to Jackson, Tennessee, that we had to reschedule her flight for two days later. That was the height of it all, when you lead your own mother astray with your drinking habits.

The alcohol express was out of control and had to be stopped, or, if not, derailed. It is all very interesting that during my crisis with the bottle, my wife had an occasional drink but never ever got close to joining me in the days of my wine and roses. I considered that she had some pretty magnificent discipline and wondered why I couldn't conjure up my own. We talked about it, and Barb convinced me I could do it for myself. What she didn't know at the time was that I was really doing it for her.

Chapter Thirty: Cold Turkey

On a cold winter morning in our College Park, Maryland, high-rise I took the oath. Not to any organization or even another individual except, of course, my wife, but just to myself. Now you have to understand that I am standing next to the chair where every evening I conducted my smoking and drinking mischief. There are two empty Rhine half-gallon bottles on the floor; I had gotten too lazy to walk to the refrigerator. A nine-inch ashtray sat beside me that was overflowing in the small space of a two-inch oval.

I vowed to quit drinking and smoking at that very moment and have never touched either since. My reasoning was that I had never been able to have just one drink. Therefore, I would never be able to taper off my drinking. My friend who died often said he admired me for this, but to me it was the only way to go if I was to stop drinking. Since this epiphany was staring me right in the face in its most abrupt way, I knew I had to deal with it, and it must be done right now. Today!

Okay, once in Acapulco at Senior Frog's I was in a dance line, and as it progressed under this guy standing on a chair he dripped tequila in people's mouths as they passed; either that or on their heads. It was a surprise, since I had no idea what he was pouring, but even sober I was game for fun. Only did it once, and it really didn't taste that good. But later, for the most part it was as my former boss at the publishing company put it, "You sure are boring when you're sober." I was able to improve this over the years.

It took a few days before the cobwebs cleared and I was able to think clearly. It would actually take three or four weeks for the fog to go away completely. And then I found myself in a new predicament, what to do with the time in the evening when I had been drinking and had crawled into my own little world. My wife and I worked together all day so there was not much left to talk about. We watched television together but we tired of that soon. Interesting was the fact that not once did I want a drink or cigarette.

I had found that discipline that Barb told me I had. And I also learned later that she had been at her wits end when I told her I agreed with her that I should do something about my drinking. The cold-turkey approach hadn't occurred to either of us at the time, and I had only arrived at this conclusion when I remembered an earlier instance before Barb and I were married. I had stopped for a couple weeks while still living in Des Moines and started back when invited to a party with friends. Didn't work.

The drink card library was pretty much history at this point, except we had an apartment full of printed-up drink cards and booze of almost every variety. Our partner took the cards and part of the booze; we saved some for parties. It was then that we began to consider returning to California, although we had no idea what we might do to earn a living. Whatever it was, it would be better than doing it in Maryland, so we talked to my Mom, and she agreed to help us in the move.

It was time to say goodbye to our partner, and it wasn't a particularly genial parting, since he thought we should stay there and keep trying to make Nasty Jack a household word. I allowed as how there was nothing I would rather do at the time, but the writing had been on the wall for a while. It said to pack it in. We did, and with Bekins to help us move, headed west again for the promised land. I was feeling better by the week now, and would soon leave two very bad habits on the East Coast.

Settled in Woodland Hills, California, in a typical La La land apartment complex, I did some consulting, and Barb worked for Kelly Girl. My Mom had always said that when she died she wanted her ashes spread in California. Now here she was in the solid state, so we suggested that we show her around as much as possible; the first thing we tried was Disneyland. She loved "It's a Small World," although getting her on and off the ride was a challenge because of her hip pain.

The drinking environment was no different in California than in Maryland, except it was a much more pleasant place to do it in. Interestingly, I wasn't drawn to the booze, and there was always the supply handy we had brought from our College Park apartment. The farther away I got from that day, giving up my two most favorite habits, the stronger I felt, although it was often necessary to remember just why I was doing this. But that's what they were, just habits, and the worst of habits can be broken.

How many years did it take me to develop the habits of drinking and smoking? Let's start with trolling the family parties where most of the guests were willing to give me a sip of their cocktail at age five. And while still in grammar school, the rendezvous with the gypsies, yielding a full pack of smokes. This transitioned into occasionally slipping a beer from my parents' stash and paying guys old enough to buy me cigarettes. By high school there was an open pipeline for both of my dirty habits.

The sub-title to this book is "How I Learned to Love My Brown Martini," and maybe that's at least part of the answer for many of you out there that may think your recreational imbibing has gotten out of hand. The Internet is the first place you should look for information. Google "am I drinking too much alcohol," and you will find some excellent sites like AlcoholScreening.org. I took a simple test using the numbers from my old habits and failed miserably. Try it.

But back to my alcohol surrogate, which I discovered along the way with the help of an expert of the coffee bean and its special selections. He founded a mail order coffee company in Southern California, and I met him in the hopes of doing some consulting work. We went out to lunch, and I expected him to order a special brew and tell me how it tasted in comparison to what he sold. Well, he told me a lot about his company, but he did it while consuming two martinis. Didn't bother him that I didn't drink.

It was actually a test for me, and I came through with flying colors. Even though he was gulping down one of my favorite drinks—and by the way, he was a chain smoker—I ordered refill after refill of a coffee that I was discovering was very good. I looked at his glass and my cup side by side and reasoned that this would be the way it would be as long as I was out selling. What I had to consider was how to get around the fact that although I didn't drink, I had no problem if the client did.

At the publishing company, I drank from fifteen to twenty cups of coffee a day, but that was solely for survival. We—the guzzler pack—decided on our own that when we killed an afternoon of work at a bar, the negative atmosphere from the higher ups was already bad enough. After all, how many conference-planning sessions could you have, especially when the sales meeting was still six months away? So, we disciplined ourselves to be at work by eight AM, a feat near impossible, hung over as we were.

But that was then and this is later, with my California coffee expert attempting to explain not only how they harvested coffee beans, but also how they roasted them for certain tastes. I listened and was amused over how Fred had said *I* was so boring after I quit drinking. This guy had downed three martinis and was still boring. At least he could have talked about sex or even sports, but we were now in the phase where the beans were put in the grinder and how important this stage was. I didn't care.

There would be lots of this kind of lunch in the future but thankfully, most of them weren't as dull. My former ministerial training must have somehow shone through, because in many cases the client would eventually decide to tell me their troubles. This usually required at least three drinks, sometimes never getting around to lunch, and leading to the necessity at times for me to deliver the person to his wife smashed. I quit scheduling dinners, because lunches never seemed to end.

Chapter Thirty-One: The Imbibery Goes On, and On, and On

One guy wanted to explain to me the details of his sex life with his wife and…his girlfriend. He was the general manager of this Los Angeles manufacturer of specialized children's toys who needed to define his market and reach the parents of kids that had this profile. He was a Manhattan dry drinker, the counterpart of the martini and just as destructive. Two toddies and he started talking. Three, and Katy unlock the door, it all came out, accompanied by a few tears.

It seems he was cheating on his wife with this girlfriend. The wife caught him and threw him out, so he moved in with the girlfriend. Now this man had to keep all this quiet from the people who owned the toy company or he could lose his job; after all, his customers were children. The girlfriend became demanding, since he was now living in her house, wanting him to spend more money on her. The wife insisted he maintain her way of life. He was caught between four legs and a "hard" place.

And then he got religion. This was just a couple weeks before our lunch, but I noted he was still scarfing down the Manhattans. We were half way through the meal now—or at least I was, he seemed to be just pushing it around—and I wondered if he would ever get to his point. I didn't have to wait much longer. He wanted me to attend a church service with him, which would be in Santa Monica, and it was the Church of Scientology. You know, L. Ron Hubbard and his preachings of Dianetics.

Hubbard began espousing this stuff in 1950, telling all his followers he could change the way they thought and improve their IQ. One has to wonder why they weren't able to help Tom Cruise. First, you had to take a Dianetics audit, then you could change your life and live it according to L. Ron Hubbard. I had run into these people when doing publicity for the publishing company at a local Channel 13 talk show in L.A. Everyone, including the show's host, walked off the set shaking their heads.

But the question was whether I should accept this guy's invitation to go with him, because I knew members got some kind of points for bringing in new suckers, and I would be taking heat the minute I walked through the door. I asked him, "What does this religious thing have to do with your personal life? And doesn't Scientology forbid drinking and smoking?" The answer was, nothing, no and no. He followed with the fact that they do forbid adultery. Now we're back to square one.

"Do you go through some kind of confession like in the Catholic Church to rid yourself of your sins?" I asked. The guy replied that it was a combination of psychotherapy and Catholic confession, involving more auditing with a church member, and it might be recorded. There's more, he said; I hold on to two V-8 cans hooked up to a contraption that measures the truth in what I say. He also had to sign a release that he wouldn't sue them. "Whoa," I told him, "this is getting way too weird for me."

I finally told my client, at the risk of losing his business, that I really wasn't a very religious person and wasn't interested in changing that any time soon. But I was still curious how this religion thing had affected the two women in his life. He told me his wife was divorcing him, and the girlfriend had thrown him out when he couldn't give her what she wanted. So the next question was, "where are you living?" The answer was, a room at the Scientology Church. The lunch ended with no closure for either of us.

It wasn't tough at all having lunch with a guy drinking Manhattans, really, not even if he had been having a martini. When I make up my mind to something as important as this, I stick to it. Believe me, it helps to have a wife who understands both sides of the problem and stands behind you all the way. Actually, Barb wasn't behind me, she was way ahead of me most of the time. However, the question arose in my mind on several occasions whether or not I should try just a couple drinks. Not, I decided.

I had been chastised regularly for drinking too much. Especially just before the end in Maryland when I invoked the cold turkey. I never thought I would run into a situation where there would be a legitimate need for me to drink. I'm not talking about an urge, but actually a justifiable reason that I should imbibe. It happened in Virginia, right outside the District. As a last-ditch effort for Nasty Jack, we hired a consultant to raise money for the drink card library who introduced us to the owner of a bourbon distillery.

Danny, the consultant, Barbara, and I went to this gentleman's home in a Virginia suburb with rocking chairs on the front porch and people sitting in them. The distiller buildings looked like something out of the old Jack Daniels ads. We mounted the steps to this typical Southern country home, and Danny introduced us to our hosts, Elwood and Abigail. Both were very gracious, and Elwood beckoned us to sit down in more rocking chairs. Danny opened the conversation by inquiring into the latest on the distillery.

Elwood allowed as how they were having a good year talking about some recent upgrades that had been made, which were not apparent from the looks of the buildings where he made his booze. Neither Elwood nor Abigail were dressed as if they lived an affluent lifestyle. From my Southern upbringing, I noticed a distinct comparison in Abigail's contribution to the conversation. She rarely spoke unless spoken to. She did stand up shortly and offered us some cookies but nothing to drink.

And then it happened. Elwood turned to me and said, "How do you like your bourbon, with water, 7UP, Coke, or what? Holy shit, Danny obviously hadn't told the man that I didn't drink and I knew Barb didn't like bourbon. But we were here to ask him for money, and how could we turn down his booze if we expected to get the backing we needed? Danny looked at me pleadingly as if to say, can't you just make this one exception? I looked at Barb, who looked bewildered.

It was probably the decision that sunk the drink card library, but I remained true to my conviction to stop drinking. What Elwood didn't know and what Danny perhaps didn't understand was that I wouldn't stop with just one drink, or two, or three. That was what the perplexed look on Barb's face was, because she admitted she could have stomached the bourbon with coke for the money. The tension between the three of us had come to a peak, but Elwood was just sitting there waiting for a drink order.

"My wife and I hate to turn down your hospitality, particularly such great Bourbon, but I quit drinking and so has she to support me." Elwood looked like he had been tasered, and Danny withdrew as if I had been the one that tasered him. I wondered what would have happened if I had said, "no thanks, I don't drink bourbon, I drink Scotch." It also occurred to me later that if I hadn't refused the drink, our host would not only have turned us down but thrown us out after I had several drinks.

Chapter Thirty-Two: I Am Not a Man of the Cloth

I can't even remember the name of the bourbon, but I do remember it was considered by many as one of the best. We left the plantation, but not until Abigail had offered Barb and me soda, and Danny had one bourbon cocktail with Elwood. The conversation veered away from why we were there and onto things about the industry of distilled spirits and how the government was planning more controls. It never returned to the purpose of our visit and we exited in defeat.

Our partner was pissed at me, and that was one of the reasons our leaving for California was not so cordial. In the meantime, Danny had decided we no longer needed his services and that was okay, since we didn't have the money to pay him anyway. But we had such plans for the drink card library; why not, we had a great name that would have been marketable. One thing we thought of was Nasty Jack Hors d'oeuvre saloons that served snacks with the NJ line of drinks. Still think it's a good idea.

So, here we were in sunny California with the drink cards behind us and who knew what before us. We had no idea what to expect in our future. This time we headed for the West Valley of Los Angeles, ending up in Woodland Hills apartments. We would work out of there for a while, with Barb doing some more Kelly Girl jobs and me a consulting job with a large manufacturer of calculating tools. My Mom was still with us and she had finally been able to get to her beloved California.

She always said that when she died she wanted her ashes spread somewhere in California, but never expected to live there in the interim. We usually took her out to dinner with us on weekends if she was feeling up to it. Of course, I wasn't drinking now, so I could escort the ladies out to do their imbibing, with me the designated driver. This would be an ongoing thing and I still serve as the teetotaler of choice behind the wheel, no matter who the drinkers are.

On one weekend following our settling in L.A. we decided to go out and celebrate the fact that we had returned to our state of choice, and we headed for a new restaurant that Barb had researched. It was typical California with a great bar and lots of comfortable red leather booths. They were, however, too cozy for my eighty-two year old mom, who proceeded to try a martini and settle in with yet another one before dinner. At home later, trying to get in bed, she broke her ankle and had to go to the hospital.

Barb's parents liked coming to L.A. to visit us but normally stayed in a hotel because we had limited space. Back in Chicago, the four of us had gone out together for dinner on several occasions and had one hell of a time. I enjoyed going out with them more than I did our friends. But in Maryland, once after an evening of boozing on New Year's Eve, Barb's Mom and I were caught in the kitchen making peanut butter and onion sandwiches. That's after she had helped put my tipsy mother to bed.

During the first occasion when they were coming to L.A., we spent rip-roaring evenings in Marina del Rey, Barb's and my favorite for fun. It was only minutes from where we lived. But the second time we moved to California we were in Woodland Hills at the end of the West Valley and miles from their airport hotel. I wasn't drinking, and they were much more sedate in their drinking habits, but we still had fun. Don't get me wrong, neither my mother nor Barb's parents made a habit of over indulging.

I was reminded of my semi-religious background one night when Barb and I were out for dinner in the Valley, and afterward we decided to go into the restaurant's piano bar and listen to some music. In those days, I was drinking coffee while she had a drink; hadn't yet progressed to sparkling water. This particular night there was a lady at the next table, with two other ladies throwing down the drinks, with a concerned look on her face, who kept looking at me. Barb noticed it, too, and began to wonder what was going on.

Suddenly the woman turned to me and said, "Father, would you take my confession?" And without letting me answer, she got up from her table and moved to ours and sat down. Barb and I were both stunned with both the suddenness and her question, until both of us realized I had on a turtleneck with a white ring around the collar, like a cleric's. But she didn't give me time to answer and pressed right on into her admissions. All I could do was listen until she finished and went back to her drinking.

Kiddingly, Barb and I commiserated over my returning to the religion business, and I related a story of what had cinched my leaving. While studying for the Methodist ministry at Lambuth College in Jackson, Tennessee, I was given a circuit of three churches to serve in the Tennessee backcountry. On one Sunday, my first wife-to-be and I left to "ride" the circuit, as preachers did years ago. Except, in lieu of a horse, we drove a 1939 Chevrolet coupe that was the church's company car.

My first two charges were uneventful, the sermon received with a reception you might expect on a hot, humid summer day in a church without air conditioning. All the windows were open and most of the attention was directed to the out-of-doors where everyone probably wished they were. I began to think I should just move outside and preach through one of the windows. It was the third church that would help shape my destiny, and serve as the deciding factor for me to leave the Methodist ministry.

I was half way through the sermon when my attention was drawn to a man to my left, on the aisle, sitting about three feet from an open window. He was furiously chewing tobacco and about every five minutes or so he would spit his wad out the window. The man was such a perfect shot that I became fascinated with the action and lost my place in the sermon. The congregation hardly noticed my interruption, probably having drifted off even earlier, wishing they were home and cool.

It was on that day that I decided that if my concentration on God's word was so poor that this tobacco exhibitionist could divert my attention that easily, and the group to which I was speaking was apparently even less interested in what I was saying than I, it was time to pack it in. Barb and I laughed at this while observing the woman who had sought my confession had quickly ordered another drink. From the looks of the rest of the table, they would all need priests tomorrow.

However, my fascination for religion has never waned, and over the years I have made a habit of reading as much on the subject as possible. When they discovered the "God Particle," I couldn't get enough of the coverage. I had an extended argument with someone at an online site; he was an atheist, I, an agnostic. We never came to any conclusion, and I still have a problem with complete unbelievers that can't adequately explain to me how the creation of man happened through pure science.

Chapter Thirty-Three: Booze Can Neutralize Racism

First, just one more story of the kind that would drive one to drink, but we have to return to Norfolk, Virginia, when I was serving on Shore Patrol. Eventually they assigned me to ride with a sergeant on the Princess Anne County patrol because so much of their action was dealing with sailors. On a Friday, we were patrolling a section of Highway One on the East Coast several years before the freeway system. Drunk swabbies seemed to proliferate on this stretch, and this evening was no different.

The Sergeant and I headed for an accident that was reported as being very serious with fatalities. The major problems here were speeding and driving drunk, and most of the time a combination of the two. This particular night was the most gruesome I have ever spent in my life. At our destination two cars had collided head on, and the Sergeant called for medics and backup as we began to hunt for survivors. During those days in the Navy there was no real training for Shore Patrol, and certainly not for this.

Both cars were packed with sailors, many of them dead, most of the others unconscious, except for one sprawled on the highway bleeding profusely. The Sarge told me to do what I could for him while he looked after the others. I can take about anything, but this guy's stomach was split open and his intestines were lying on the ground. He was begging for help, and I was sure from his condition, and the way he looked at me, that he really knew he had no chance.

I immediately got on the ground, put his head in my lap, and tried to console him. Then he pleaded with me to put his guts back inside his body while telling me he didn't want to die. I tried with some success but just moments later he died. I stayed with him until help arrived because I couldn't stand for his head to lie on the cold ground. The Navy medics said there was no way he could have survived. It is a picture I will never be able to get out of my mind, but one I would hope would deter potential drunk drivers.

While living in Jackson, Tennessee, the family made trips to visit relatives in Fulton, Kentucky, and Como, Mississippi. I'll never forget Fulton because of a couple of hack surgeons who removed my appendix in a hastily arranged surgery at the last minute, just after they had been drafted for WWII. They left me with an incision of heavy scar tissue about one-half inch wide, which I still have. It took forever to heal and kept me from playing football.

Fulton was my first experience with anti-Semitism. There was a girl I really liked named Carmel, who was Jewish, and whose father owned a mercantile store there. We were too young to date, but she did invite me over to her house. The family seemed to accept me, but then, of course, we were far from the serious age. One day, when I told the gentile owner of the department store where my grandmother worked how much I liked Carmel, he reacted with disdain, saying this was not proper for a Christian boy like me.

Even at that age, I told him I didn't care, and what did "not proper" mean, anyway? He just looked at my mother and grandmother saying, "You really have a problem there." I started questioning him again and was promptly cut off by my mother. Somehow my parents had instilled in me—although I don't actually remember the exact coaching—that all people were equal. Now this made sense to me and was the reason I could see nothing wrong with having Carmel as a girlfriend.

More on prejudice...Como was farther south in what was considered the Mississippi Delta: rich farmland that produced luscious crops of cotton, corn and peas. My uncle on my father's side had two 500-acre plantations that were managed by a black man, for whom I had a great deal of admiration. They called him "Man," and to this day I don't recall his real name. He also worked as the butcher at my uncle's grocery store, and I could see from his customers the high regard the white community had for him.

I will never forget our conversations—he didn't talk about race, even though racism was raging in the South in those days—but just about life and how a young man like me should live it. There wasn't a bitter bone in Man's body. While wrestling with the racial situation in the South, I would look at Man, then at my father and mother, then my uncle and aunt, knowing that his color was different. "But what difference did that make?" was a question that I earnestly asked myself. None, to me.

One day I asked him, "Man, why do you always come to the back door of my uncle's house, rather than the front?" He answered, "Mr. Jack, that's the way we do it down here and I really don't mind. Mr. Ray (my uncle) respects me and I respect myself, so no harm is done." Man could have been the poster person for Martin Luther King's campaign for racial equality. Once I asked him about the "N" word, blurting it out before I realized. He replied that black folks had just learned to live with it. Terrible, I thought.

In the early 1960s our family of five traveled from Los Angeles to Memphis for a vacation, then down to Como to visit my uncle and aunt. A quick story about my Aunt Sallie, who was a corker, just the opposite of her brother, my father, who was all business. As an example, whenever Aunt Sallie didn't like what you were saying, she simply turned off her hearing aid, and you might as well stop talking. But all her friends understood, and just kept talking, which made her happy.

When we left the Tennessee line and entered Mississippi, I noticed a helicopter overhead. It followed us all the way to Como, and when there, I asked my uncle what it could be. He called a friend on the highway patrol and was told they had mistaken us for racial demonstrators, based on our California plates. Now this pissed me off, and I wondered how much this prejudiced state spent on this kind of racist surveillance. This was in the late 1950s, just before all racial hell broke loose in the South.

Regarding race, California wasn't like that in the 1970s, although it had had and still did have its racial problems. The Watt's riots were earlier, and the back of my company car had taken a hit when I got too close to the area on a freeway while visiting a client, and a bullet went through the rear window. And then there was Rodney King in the 1990s, who was stopped in a high-speed chase, beaten by police in a scuffle. When they were acquitted in court, it started the worst race riot in American history.

You could live in L.A. side by side with blacks with absolutely no problems, but when something like King or Watts occurred, it seemed to bring out the worst in everyone. Even close friends of a different color were leery and avoided each other until everything had quieted down. It's hard to figure out who was wrong in those days, but it's likely there was enough blame for both sides. Even up until today, this country has not learned to deal with racial tensions.

And then Barack Obama was elected President in 2008, winning reelection for a second term, which kinda augured that the country had decided on the racial issue, since Obama is black. Not so. As a matter of fact, it might have even made it worse with groups like the Tea Party openly expressing racist behavior against the President. These people didn't vote for the man, and since his election have led a movement to impeach Barack Obama, even trying to prove his birth certificate was invalid.

There is a connection between gun control and racism. An Australian study found racial resentment increases the odds that a person will have a gun in the house, and still be opposed to gun control. It found that more than any other racial group, whites opposed restrictions on having guns, which is explained in part by a prejudice against blacks. Throughout history, governments have professed that gun control laws were useful for keeping blacks and Hispanics "in their place" and for quieting the racial fears of whites.

But the United States is not unique in its racial tendencies, as evidenced by four other similar nations. The United Kingdom, in general, is up four percent in recent years in its prejudice toward those of color. In France, racial slurs are more common and even accepted. Germany's Constitutional law prevents it but is not enforceable, and blacks are the ones first approached for drugs. Canadians explain it as the old against the new, with minorities now getting more attention from government.

The question arises, if I grew up in a racially bigoted South, and most of those around me, including family, were prejudiced against blacks, why didn't I adopt the same views? Was there a difference in my genes or something in the water that I drank? Not likely, but if not, how do you explain someone's radical views over a humanitarian attitude like this as compared to another person in the exact same environment, not sharing those views?

And what does all this have to do with drinking? Some people turn into everyone's friend when they are inebriated, and others become a nasty drunk. I was one of the former, and most of my drinking friends were the same. On one particular evening I was imbibing with one of these friends who was very prejudiced against blacks, and we were very drunk. In walks another friend of mine, black, and the three of us spent an extremely amicable evening that definitely was not an act by my white friend.

I am neither suggesting that alcohol should be used to improve race relations, nor am I implying that whites should always drink while around blacks, and vice versa. Fully realizing the effects of booze in my years of imbibing, one of my reasons for picking up a drink was to relax and get my mind off problems; that is, until I learned to love the taste. It is a well-known fact that liquor can curb inhibitions, so I often wonder if that friend of mine might not have been as prejudiced as he thought he was.

Chapter Thirty-Four: Does Sobriety Equal Boring?

After I had given up the grape, and once when I returned to Des Moines on a business trip, I spent some time one evening with my former boss at the publishing company. After several minutes of conversation, and after Fred had consumed half of his martini, he made an interesting statement. He said, "You know, Jack, since you quit drinking, you're boring." At first I wasn't sure how to reply but finally retorted, "Well, at least now you can understand what I am saying."

We spent another hour or so talking over old times, laughing over incidents like the time the two of us were driving back from working in San Diego to my home in Huntington Beach. We were scheduled to take my wife out to dinner, had had a liquid lunch, and were eating tacos on the way. Of which I proceeded to drop parts into my lap, requiring a change of clothes before going back out. The slob in me when I eat has perpetuated over the years, even persevering until this day.

The dinner was a disaster, and my wife was pissed at me for several days. The highlight of the evening was when Fred and I debated the advantages of whether or not to eat the potato skin, trying to determine how many nutrients were in this brown casing. We even brought the waitress into what had become a full blown controversy. She passed the problem around the kitchen and reported to us later that even the chef did not know. Fred and I looked at each other, said "what the hell" and had another drink.

Back in a sober Des Moines, Fred and I were reminiscing over drunken conversations while he finished his second martini. Noticing him beginning to slur his words, I realized that was the first stage of plastered speech, a phase I went through regularly in the past on the way to oblivion. I suggested food. Fred suggested another drink. It was good to know he felt comfortable imbibing with an old drinking buddy, who no longer drank. I found out what I had sounded like, which gave me the idea for this book.

Nevertheless, I had always considered myself a pretty good conversationalist, at least holding my own in a group, but now had some doubts about participating in a fully sober exchange. Had I been that drunk for that long? I turned to Barb for some consolation in my dilemma and she told me I was a very interesting person, smashed or sober, which made me feel better for a time. Until I realized she would support me no matter what, although she wouldn't outwardly mislead me.

What I did notice in this new state of sobriety was that I could be confrontational when discussing certain subjects like politics and religion. I am an agnostic and a progressive liberal, converting some years ago from the bleeding variety. After a few drinks I might be able to concede that George W. Bush wasn't the worst President ever, but with me off the sauce, his position there was a non-negotiable certainty, and to argue with me could provoke some challenges, which I later might regret.

At times I fear I might have been talking down to some people, because it appeared to me they didn't have their facts straight. Not that I am always right. It is simply that I make it a point to never get involved in a heated discussion over a subject that I have not read about thoroughly. At the same time, I can be very quick to admit that I am wrong about something if that is the case. The huge difference here is that after throwing down three martinis, most don't care *who* is right or wrong.

Now it is over thirty-five years later, and my friend's statement still comes up occasionally. I don't believe I have developed a complex over the matter, but often think back to my drinking bouts and try to remember how I might have been talking just prior to launching into my happy stupor. Never having come up with an answer, I can only assume that what came out was a special kind of gibberish that only drunks understand. And, it is only available to those who are bombed out of their minds.

However, being boring has its advantages, according to the man who puts on a Boring Conference. That's right, James Ward brings "boring" people together for the purpose of learning what being bored does to and says about the average person. To me, this means there is hope for all those dull boozed-up characters like my former self that haven't yet seen the light. Of course, one must make up their mind first whether they choose an inebriated oblivion or a world of sober facts.

According to Linda Rodriquez McRobbie of the Smithsonian, "boredom" first became a word in 1852 in Charles Dickens' *Bleak House*, itself considered partially boring. Dickens apparently started something, since psychologists later discovered a dark side of boredom; it can be something very similar to depression. That's it, I thought, was I really boring after giving up hooch, or was I just depressed? No doubt in my mind, I had become boring, at least for a while, without my crutch.

At one point it occurred to me that in chatting with others who were drinking while I was abstaining, trying to talk sense with someone who had downed three martinis did not in itself make sense. They didn't really want to talk, they just wanted to drink. So why should I sit there trying to solve the problems of the world while my friend simply wants to propagate the buzz he or she has developed? But not everyone subscribed to my mandate of, "Let's hurry up and get drunk."

There was the other angle. It isn't exactly entertaining to sit around and listen to someone almost zonked out who is talking in a foreign tongue. In my case, I considered it retribution for those years my dear wife and others had tolerated me. Not that my wife was ever a heavy drinker, although there were a couple times over the years when it was our decision to leave the car parked and take a cab home. In her case, however, she had never had too much to be able to drive responsibly.

If it is possible for animals to be bored, my dog, Snuffy, must have suffered an excruciating existence when we lived in Huntington Beach, California. In the late evening after I had consumed considerable vodka from bottles hidden all over the house—my favorite places included on a hanger behind the washing machine and the space just behind the front cover under the dish washing machine—I would eventually end up on the floor in the dining room conversing with man's best friend.

Snuffy loved me when I was drunk because he had my undivided attention. This was partially due to the fact that no one else in the family wanted anything to do with me, but deep down I liked spending the time with my little buddy. Later, when I had remarried, we were attending a party at the home of my wife's boss who had two Vizsla dogs who were very social. After seventy-eight drinks during the evening, I ended up on the floor schmoozing with these guys who ignored everyone else at the party.

However, my talks with other-than-humans was not limited to dogs. We had a parakeet in Maryland called Toes, named so because when my wife would let her out of her cage, she would fly over and land on my toes while I was stretched out on the couch, drinking a martini. After the second or third drink my wife swears that the bird was actually listening to what I was saying, because her head moved back and forth with each comment. And in this case, there was no doubt as to who the birdbrain was.

And that's not even all of my creature connections, although the following story could have taken a wrong turn. We adopted a feisty little tabby cat while in the same Maryland apartment, who was rescued from the sewers around Washington, D.C. LJ was hopelessly cross-eyed, a condition that didn't prevent him from getting around but made him adorable to all our friends and neighbors. The rescue group wasn't sure, but the little guy must have fought rats for his food, evidenced by a nicked ear.

LJ had the run of the apartment with his new sister, Thomasina, who came from the same rescue he did. She arrived second after being spayed. Not knowing the protocol in introducing animals then, we just put them together in the same room. It looked like they were going to kill each other, and when finally separating them, they were kept in different rooms and reintroduced gradually. Eventually, Thomasina and LJ became good friends and even slept together on a bean bag in our bedroom.

We got the kitty cats because Barb thought they would take our minds off our financial problems and was anxious to adopt from the rescue. They did their job, and we doted over them like the children they were. I still ended the evening with Scotch and usually took my drink and a cigarette to bed. The two kitties slept in our bedroom, and one night LJ decided to finish the dregs of my toddy and ended up more cross-eyed the next day. Good thing it wasn't enough to harm him.

Chapter Thirty-Five: Swapping Booze for the Brown Martini

At the writing of this book I am eighty-four years old, and reaching this age has not been easy, considering my marathon with one-fifth of Scotch a day and four packs of cigarettes at the cusp of my career. Yes, as indicated before, you can start your drinking as a hobby, pastime, or diversion. But, the more serious of us progress to larger heights, leading to a regimen and discipline that would mirror the dedication of any corporate CEO in this country. After a while, it becomes natural in your daily lifestyle.

That's when you should worry, but I never did. There was always that next drink, when you would whisk yourself off into the fantasy world of your daily swill, and believe me, it could be anything from wine to the hard stuff, with any of the frilly things like liqueurs in between. It isn't what you're drinking that counts, it's the buzz. I wonder when you and others read this if this is more common than we think. I would like to know just how many of you drink just to get drunk. Will you email me? Probably not.

My wife has commented before that she is not sure this kind of behavior means I am an alcoholic. Perhaps just someone with a very large drinking problem. So how do you differentiate between the two? Alcoholics Anonymous has twelve questions to help you determine if you need their organization. The National Council on Alcoholism and Drug Dependence has twenty-five questions to help you determine if you have an addiction to alcohol. I failed miserably on both tests.

So if I stopped my imbibing cold turkey, does that mean I was really not an alcoholic? From research, it is not a matter of whether stopping cold turkey does or does not define alcoholism. The facts are, it is not a good idea to try self de-tox, and in some cases this could prove dangerous, even fatal. At the very least you should not attempt to self de-tox at home alone, but do it under the care of a professional. Like I've said, it was the only way I could get it done. Apparently I was lucky.

My suggestion is to talk to your primary care doc. He or she should have the kind of experienced advice to put you on the right path. If you don't get what you want, call Alcoholics Anonymous or Google their site for a meeting location near you. My background, particularly with my close friend who died from alcohol abuse, tells me that when you do go to AA, you must go there with a commitment. Otherwise, your efforts could fail because of what they call, "falling off the wagon."

In the theory of the survival of the fittest, the weakest are culled on a regular basis, making the strongest even stronger. This has now been applied to the human brain, which can only operate as fast as the slowest brain cells. Everyone knows that alcohol kills brain cells; in my case, perhaps committing mass murder. But in natural selection, it attacks the weakest cells first. Therefore, in the regular consumption of beer, you get rid of your weaker brain cells, and then feel smart as hell after a few beers.

The above is taken from an anonymous quote sent to me in an email by my friend Don Klein. And yes, there is some humor in drinking if you can keep your intake under control. Following is another great poetic quote by Dorothy Parker: "I like to have a martini, two at the very most. After three I'm under the table, after four I'm under my host." F. Scott Fitzgerald said: "First you take a drink, then the drink takes a drink, then the drink takes you." The latter perfectly describes my former boozing habits.

And there is justification for the fact that I was convinced I had turned into Fred Astaire on the dance floor when my wife and I went out on the weekend to "swing," as we called boogying. Kimberly Hayes Taylor reported on NBC, "Neuroscientists at Washington University School of Medicine in St. Louis have identified brain cells and functions that allow extremely intoxicated people to perform complex tasks such as dancing…" Then self-realization occurred; I woke up the next morning and was still me.

But now I am a card-carrying coffee drinker, replacing booze with this exquisite, tantalizing brew I call my "Brown Martini." When first meeting my wife, Barb, at the office where we both worked in Chicago, one Christmas she gave me a coffee cup that had the following imprinted on the side: "Just Think of it as a Brown Martini." That is when she first experienced my heavy drinking and probably was trying to send me a message. It is also where I got the sub-title for this book.

As I think back to the Sunday morning when I said to myself, this is it, no more drinking or smoking, I remember that I suddenly became anxious, even alarmed, wondering what I would replace the booze with. I was in an alcoholic rut and needed a new crutch. Cigarettes were no problem; if I didn't drink, I didn't smoke. I sat in my chair by the patio doors all morning without coming up with an answer. I would never be hung over again, so my "Cockroach" cocktail would be a wasted effort.

We were drinking instant coffee in those days simply for the convenience and the fact that we would never consume a whole brewed pot. I went into the kitchen searching for some kind of non-alcoholic beverage, passing on a couple of kinds of soda, and then spied the instant coffee. Why the hell not, I thought, but without a microwave in those days we had to heat a kettle of water. During the process I reflected on the difference in preparing this beverage with pouring Scotch over ice. Definitely not the same.

But it tasted good, better than I experienced from coffee machines I would attack in the future when desperate for a caffeine hit. One of the worst I ever encountered was at a car wash in Ventura, California; it tasted like the soap they used to clean the cars. You have to remember that this was before Mr. Starbucks entered the picture. I don't know if Howard Schultz, Starbuck's CEO, had a vision that there were all these folks giving up booze and switching to coffee, or just identifying more coffee drinkers in the future.

Whatever his intention, he not only supplied what was to become the liquid refreshment of the day, but he also provided the perfect ambiance in which to drink it. I personally think their coffee is too strong and my wife agrees, something about the roasting, I'm told, but that doesn't prevent us from making several trips to the round green-and-white sign each week. As a matter of fact, I have written a preponderance of one novel, this memoir, and five short stories while in a number of Starbucks locations.

I thrive on the noise around me, which seems to enhance my creativeness and produce more work. There is no doubt in my mind that this comes from my years of working nights in television while going to college. A TV control room consists of a bank of monitors and an electronic board with several buttons to select everything, from cameras in the studio to video to the network. People included an engineer, a director, and an announcer in an enclosed booth.

I was the director at the control board surrounded by these people, plus anyone that might wander over from radio, between their station breaks. There was non-stop conversation while I sat there making sure nothing went wrong on the network show we were carrying, while studying for the next day's classes. Most shows were one-half hour, so I had that long between breaks. I hit gold when the network broadcast an hour show, even two hours. It is still hard for me to concentrate today without the noise factor.

There is some scientific foundation for this, coming from Ben Greenfield Fitness, which categorizes brain wave patterns. The research says that most people live their lives in primarily beta brain waves, "...aroused, alert, concentrated, but also somewhat stressed." The other two are alpha, "Relaxation, super learning, relaxed focus, light trance, increased serotonin production." And Theta, "Dreaming (REM) sleep." Delta, "Dreamless sleep." Based on my concentration during noise, I would be an alpha.

My wife is just the opposite; she needs quiet to concentrate. But the reason I bring all this up is that, maybe not as many of my brain cells died as I thought when I was slugging it down. There are billions of neurons or nerve cells in the brain, and the question in my mind is just how many do you need to survive in the modern day environment? And then there are scientists that say alcohol does not kill brain cells, rather it damages them, especially if you drink mass amounts like I did.

Some temperance writers in an earlier period proclaimed that the alcohol in one's blood could cause boozers to catch fire and burn alive. I can see it now, around midnight in the Firebrand, right in the middle of the bar, Fred and I burst into flames, and everyone runs for their life. But some medical research has demonstrated that moderate drinkers are better able to think and reason than non-drinkers. Okay, all you wannabes, this is not an invitation to drink. The best way to go is to stay away from it. Completely.

However, the Journal of Neuroscience says that abstinence after chronic alcohol abuse does enable the brain cells to repair themselves. Once again, not a crutch, but rather a Band-Aid if you're trying to quit. The only sure solution is to quit, preferably with help. If you think you need to buttress yourself to help get you started, use meditation or yoga. With the proper supervision, you might also try self-hypnosis, all of which are readily available on the Internet. As I have counseled myself, "you do what you have to."

Chapter Thirty-Six: There is Magic in Drinking and More
Shenanigans

There is a bewitching place in Hollywood, right off the
Boulevard and just down the block from the Highlander Hotel,
my first California home. I have a very warm feeling for this
motel, partly because it was my initial stop in the Golden State
and secondly, because it was here I met the writer Bill Ballinger
and all of the great things we did there and in L.A. It turned into
a Hollywood experience for me, and it was one that I will not
only never forget but remember fondly as one of the reasons for
this book.

And now, to an enchanting place on Franklin Avenue
called the Hollywood Magic Castle. It is legendary for magicians
around the world who perform there regularly. I was there twice,
once during a junk mail convention in Los Angeles and the other
at the invitation of one of its premiere illusionists, Mark Wilson.
They have one of the finest restaurants in the city and one of the
most fascinating bars in the country. It is there where the special
attraction is that attracts thousands of visitors.

If you enter the bar and take the stool second from the
end, you expect to sit down and have your favorite drink and
converse with your friend and companion. What you suddenly
realize, especially if you are sober, is that the bar stool very
slowly sinks to the floor. Your first inclination is that you must
be slouching and your partner is sitting up straight. Then it gets
worse, and a mild case of panic sets in because you know
something is happening, but not what. Then the bartender shows
you a button to right the stool.

It's a great stunt, especially if the person next to you
doesn't know what's going on. In my case, during the convention
when a crowd of us were there, the guy I was sitting next to did,
but I didn't. We sat down for a drink after already downing many
at the hotel, my friend guiding me to the trickster stool. Halfway
through my martini I noticed this guy, who was already tall, had
grown at least a foot. He, of course, acted as if nothing was

178

happening looking down at me like you would at your small child.

Along came the second martini, and I noticed my associate was turning into a giant. During this time he was waving off the bartender to not tell me about the secret button. When I was looking at a pair of knees, even in my inebriated state it was obvious that something was wrong with this picture. It all became quite obvious when I turned the stool slightly and was looking into the faces of a bunch of snickering people, most of which I didn't know. Such are the perils of serious drinking.

The other big secret of the Castle is a urinal in the men's room, which plays "It's a Small World" when you stand in front of it. Not very good for the ego but does provoke laughter from everyone in the room.

Some of the members winning their "magician of the Year" award are: Mark Wilson, Siegfried & Roy, Doug Henning, Harry Blackstone Jr., David Copperfield, Harry Anderson, Lance Burton, Penn & Teller, David Blaine, and others. Some won twice or more. A fantastic place to visit if you can get invited.

Back in nineteen seventy-seven and half way across the country from the Magic Castle someone had an answer for drunk drivers. For only twenty-five cents the drinking customers of Des Moines' Office Lounge could find out if they had had too much to drink to drive. This was, of course, after my stint there, and I am not even sure patrons of the Firebrand would have made use of the contraption. However, they could have put it on the wall beside the condom machines and just hope for the best.

Although I didn't know it then, my destiny would be to create memorable scenarios for the future. When I first came up with this wacky idea right after giving up drinking, my initial thought was the title, "Without the Lampshade," which I connected with drunks with lampshades on their heads. It was a caricature that had been used over the years, depicting happy imbibers, of which I was certainly one. Like most of my ideas on writing, they have remained dormant over the years for one reason or another.

And then things started happening—as accounted for in this book—and somehow I knew that one day I would put it all down on paper. The funny thing is that even as the book develops, I think of events and throw them in during the work in progress, hoping you won't object to this kind of presentation. One such re-remembered episode happened in Detroit while working for the Chicago data center. As I said earlier, the management of this company was the epitome of the Peter Principle, incompetence exaggerated.

Well, this particular trip to the Motor City, the firm's headquarters, was to be for the purpose of training, and the evidence of ineptitude was even more prevalent here. Now don't get me wrong, this company had some excellent talent, but I seemed to run into the bunglers rather than the producers. I was with several guys, one of which was also from the Chicago office. We'll call him Dave, and the guy was young, single, and very horny. He was a good man who needed guidance, which he would never get.

A few of us went out for drinks the first night in town, Dave included, and late in the evening ended up at a bar in downtown Detroit. As we walked in the door, Dave was immediately scrutinizing the crowd for a potential pickup. The rest of us sat down and ordered drinks after having downed several earlier at the hotel. It wasn't long until Dave returned to the table with his score, a very attractive lady from Flint, Michigan, married but alone, and seventy-one years old. That's right, a senior citizen.

She was already on her way, and we all ordered another round, then another, yet another. Now there are some appealing seventy-year old women, and today I wouldn't question Dave's reasoning. But then all I could say was, "Dave, are you out of your fucking mind with all these good looking younger women here?" Although I had heard what he was about to say several times before, this was the first time it actually registered with me. Dave said simply, "She's nice looking and for her, every time is the last time."

He departed with Ms. Flint Michigan, and the rest of us had one more drink. My drinking buddies decided to catch a cab back to the hotel; I decided to walk. Well I did, right through the worst part of downtown Detroit with the potential of a desperate druggie on every corner. It wasn't long until the sheer darkness around me, highlighted by closed-down, dilapidated buildings began to sober me up, instilling some real fear. And then suddenly I saw the lighted tower of our hotel and headed home. Lucky again.

We were in meetings all the next morning, and just before lunch, Dave came up to me and told me of the call he had received from Ms. Flint Michigan. It seemed some of her very expensive jewelry was missing and she came to the conclusion Dave had taken it. The two of us went quickly to her hotel room and the lady was beside herself, since the necklace and bracelet were from her husband. She told Dave to cough it up or she was calling the police, and I could tell that she meant it. She was not going to calm down.

We talked and I tried to soothe things, but the woman was having none of it. She was convinced Dave was the culprit and was about to make her call to the cops when I said, "Why didn't you put your jewelry in the hotel safe?" First, she had a perplexed look on her face, then said, "Oh shit," and headed to the heating unit just under the window. When she pulled up the cover for the controls, she found her bracelet and necklace. Apologies were in order as well as an offer for aménage á trois, but lunch was over.

In case you're interested, according to Christopher Beam of Slate online, lampshades on the head became the "universal symbol of drunkenness" in around the 1910s to 1920s. And in later years it embodied "the obnoxious drunk trying to be funny—and failing." French philosopher Henri Bergson says simply, a standing lamp resembles the form of a person, only a shade instead of the head. Another take, a drunk guy leaves a party and grabs a lampshade instead of his hat.

Not once did I ever put a lampshade on my head. To begin with, in my regular drunken narcosis, there would never have been the acuity to unscrew the knob necessary to get the damn thing off the lamp. But somehow when the subject of drinking comes up, the natural inclination of many is to picture the guy with a lampshade on his head. I have never seen a woman with a lampshade on her head and do not know what significance this has to the fable. Is drinking male chauvinistic?

For many years Bill Hoest's cartoon in the Sunday papers, "The Lockhorns," represented the archetype drinker, Leroy. While viewing the cartoon weekly I related to Leroy, in particular when his wife, Lois, would look at him in the morning while pouring him a cup of coffee and say, "Maybe you'd better list who you want as pall bearers." And finally Leroy's reply to stopping drinking, "Why should I take the cure when the disease is more fun?"

Chapter Thirty-Seven: Busted at a Bar and Some More Final
Recollections

My wife and I were at a bar one night with friends, and
the guy's wife happened to drink as much as I did. We had
planned to eat later, but in the meantime proceeded to get
plastered. My wife and the gal's husband held back because they
were the designated "least drunk" drivers. During the course of
the evening the decision was made to replace dinner with some
hors d'oeuvres in the bar. When the food came we decided to
ditch the hard stuff and switch to wine.

Our waitress brought two decanters of wine and four
glasses and poured for all of us. We ate and we drank, but the
booze won out in my case and that of our friend's wife. In other
words, we remained bashed and ready for just about anything. I
suggested that she put one of the empty wine decanters in her
purse as a souvenir for the evening. She did, and eventually our
drink fest was over and we decided to leave. Well, we were met
at the front door by the manager and forced to give up our prize.
Very, very embarrassing.

The publishing company where I worked had regular
sales conferences, some in Des Moines at the home office,
covered in an earlier chapter, and others at more exotic locations
like Sarasota, Florida. At this particular event I had recently been
promoted to sales manager, and when Fred and I arrived early,
became immediately aware of the great possibilities of this place
to relax the guys, but unfortunately did not recognize the
downside of an ocean only feet from the back door of the resort.

We had the usual hospitality suite stocked to the gunnels
with booze and plenty of room to play card games and roll dice.
This particular evening we had had a great dinner with a guest
who was a famous writer who also had a home in Sarasota.
Later, while playing cards and still somewhat sober, one of my
men got up from the table and said, "I'm going for a swim."
Someone else sat in and we played a couple of hands, when it

suddenly dawned on me what the guy had said. He was going for a swim.

By then it was almost midnight, and I knew the pool was closed, and as drunk as this guy was, something told me he wasn't going for the pool, he would be headed for the ocean. I knew there could be riptides but didn't know if they were prevalent now. I ran out the back door of the hotel screaming his name and ran toward the surf. Fortunately, there was a full moon and I could see its trail of light into the beach. And there was my guy, walking toward the moon as if he planned to get there.

I "rescued" him from about fifty feet into the water by just grabbing his arm and turning both of us around, heading back to the beach. He acted as if he was just out for a stroll, not realizing the significance of what might have happened had his journey continued. We were both soaked to the waist, and although none of the other salesmen had seen the incident, it was obvious something had happened when we walked through the lobby. I escorted him to his room and told him to go to bed.

Later in my drinking career—and it did seem like my life's work at the time, with the effort I devoted to it—I learned that you could become a gourmet cook if you drank just enough in the process to be creative. I had bought several cookbooks from *Gourmet* magazine as well as *Larousse Gastronomique* and *A Treasury of Great Recipes* by Mary and Vincent Price. I studied over these volumes judiciously as I downed my daily bottle of Scotch, fortified with several packs of cigarettes.

And on one very hung-over morning I decided that, enough of the cramming, I was now ready to become the chef that I was always meant to be, at least according to the rules of "one part water, ten parts Scotch" law. It is amazing what booze can do for the psyche. In some cases it can provoke a person into violence. In this case it only awakened my culinary talents, which I hadn't known were there and wouldn't have been without the toddy. It would all start with that afternoon's drink and smoke fest.

Today I would prepare a roasted jalapenos soup for my mother, who was living with us at the time, and me. My wife was out of town visiting her family in Chicago, and had she been at home, this catastrophe would never have happened. But it did, based on my remembrances from the use of the jalapenos in a wide range of recipes when we lived in California. Of course, the people preparing these dishes weren't smashed and handled the peppers with the utmost caution. I didn't.

Jalapenos are hot, not only to eat, but also to the touch, due to the capsaicin. I apparently didn't read that part of the recipe and jumped right into the preparation with bare hands, a drink and a cigarette close by. There were also onions, carrots, tomatoes and garlic in the soup that had to prepared. After working through that and at least a couple more drinks and several cigarettes, I began to feel heat in my fingers. First, just a little, then it got worse and worse. At least the soup was simmering away.

Looking back at the recipe, although with a tipsy point of view, I noticed the instructions to use some kind of gloves when cutting and peeling the jalapenos. I hadn't, but at least now the alcohol was decreasing the feelings in my hands and I either wasn't feeling it as much or didn't give a damn. Finally the soup was done, and my mother came to the table and we sat down. I was barely able to negotiate the chair, took one spoonful, and went back in the kitchen and made us two peanut butter and jelly sandwiches.

It is interesting that after I stopped drinking, which was not too long after this gala dinner, the desire to cook disappeared and is still gone to this day. There is no doubt that a good psychologist would have a field day with this behavior, probably tracing it back to some quirky relationship with my mother as a child. She was a very good cook and had her specialties, but never, ever, encouraged me to cook. Whatever it was, I still love to eat to this day, but leave the cooking up to my very capable wife.

As we move away from the days of wine and roses, there was one family occasion that reminded me of the old days. It was our granddaughter's wedding in Des Moines, with several members of the family there I didn't even know, or at least remember, if I did. Guess the reason is that I hate reunions and never attend them if there is any way to avoid them. As George Burns said, "Happiness is having a large, loving, caring, close-knit family in another city."

At the wedding, however, things were different and no one was bored. Unfortunately, the marriage didn't last, but this day was filled with renewing family acquaintances, even some old friends from Des Moines, and at least our granddaughter was happy for the moment. There wasn't a lot of drinking going on, but what there was consisted of only beer and wine. I ended the day dancing to several songs with my son, which was a real crowd pleaser but a sober reminder of the past.

In the last few years I have had a problem with my balance, sometimes severe. Guess I couldn't drink booze even if I wanted to, unless I would be willing to take a flight of stairs head first. I can see the look on my neurologist's face now. Sheer horror when I tell her, "Oh, by the way, in addition to my lousy equilibrium, I consume a fifth of Scotch a day." The doc is understanding, but I can't see her budging on this issue. She knew about my drinking past, just shaking her head when I told her.

A lot of my doctors have done this, so I make it a point to qualify my foregone bad habits with the fact that I haven't had any pop or cigarettes for over thirty years, and the fact that when I realized what this was doing to me, I quit both cold turkey. Does that make me a star or a hero? Hell, no. It just means that this is the way I do things. Make up my mind, often based on facts related to the issue, then scare up the discipline with which to do it. It worked. By the way, it also helped me eliminate my motion sickness.

Hopefully, those with this problem will have a spouse, or at least someone close like I did, for support in their sojourn to sobriety. I would not be here today if it weren't for my wife, Barbara. My liver not only survived, but today is in much better shape than I deserve. I owe it to her for giving me the will to do what I did and being my cornerstone with which to do it. Regarding my current balance problems, she now refers to me as a "sober drunk." Yes, we both still have a good sense of humor.

Made in the USA
Lexington, KY
05 September 2016